The Hopelessly Human Nurse

The Hopelessly Human Nurse

simple strategies for overhauling your lamp

Linda Bridge and Kathy Knowles

Illustrations by Rosalie Wilson

Illustrations by Rosalie Wilson

Published by
Hopelessly Human Productions Inc.
Box 1092, Lethbridge, Alberta, Canada T1J 4A2

Additional copies of this book may be ordered from this address and via our web site — www.hopelesslyhuman.ca..

Printed in Canada by The Warwick Printing Co. Ltd., Lethbridge, AB.
First Printing: Feb, 2005
Second Printing: June, 2005

Library and Archives Canada Cataloguing in Publication Data:

Bridge, Linda, 1958-

The hopelessly human nurse: simple strategies for overhauling your lamp

Linda Bridge & Kathy Knowles; illustrations by Rosalie Wilson.

Includes bibliographical references.

ISBN 0-9736040-0-X

1. Nursing. I. Knowles, Kathy, 1959- II. Title.

RT82.B745 2004 610.73 C2004-906590-4

This book is intended to serve as a catalyst for positive change. It is not intended to be, and should not be relied upon, as a substitute for competent individual medical, psychiatric, psychological or psycho-therapeutic advice, or other professional counselling. Neither the authors nor the publisher by this book are, or purport to be, engaged in rendering medical, psychiatric, psychological, psycho-therapeutic advice, or are engaged in professional counselling of any nature or kind whatsoever.

The authors and publisher disclaim all responsibility for any claim, loss, damages, or liability, personal or otherwise, howsoever caused or arising, and whether arising or caused directly or indirectly, alleged to have occurred as a result of the use and application of any of the contents of this book.

To those who believe
in the art of nursing

Contents

F.I.P.*

* Foreword, Introduction and Preface, all rolled into one!

Welcome to my first pregnancy and birth of a book. Laugh if you must, but believe me, I've had all the changes; from bloating to swollen feet and hemorrhoids to heartburn. Sometimes wishing for a premature birth just to be done, then switching gears and paternally praying for a perfect child. I asked for a maternity leave of absence from work and my manager laughed at me. How rude!! Oh yeah, did I mention the mood swings?

For years I've been saying I should write a book, but I never imagined it would be one like this. I envisioned, as most nurses do, a book of events and situations we found funny or horrific. As Kathy and I started this project I started changing, realizing that although I use some of these strategies to deal with my work life issues, there were so many more. I had some 'Ah Ha' moments over the course of my writings about my life, my health, and what I wanted for myself. This defined for me what was truly a passion for the art of nursing.

It has been a thrilling exploration and I have only scratched the surface. The need to go deeper and trust myself to truly change is here.

L.B.

I once thought that if my former husband just changed this, if my son stopped doing that or if my friend quit being that way I would feel better, be better and do better.

Bravely, I faced the fact it was I who needed to change.

It was not about losing weight or dyeing my hair or buying just the right outfit. It was not about writing a best seller, climbing the corporate ladder or being in the correct social realm.

Nervously, I faced myself in the mirror. I cried and cried, realizing how angry I was at her and how unhealthy this was.

I cried and cried and began treating my mirror reflection more respectfully.

I am replacing my negative self-talk with positive accolades. I am taking responsibility for my happiness and my needs. I have and will continue to change how I communicate.

I falter, I slide back, I leap way ahead. But I respect my humanness now!

I've changed and so have those around me. I was, and still am, awed at how this happens — at the powerfulness of my simple alterations.

I believe in this power and it is this belief that led me to write this book.

I not only feel and believe, but I know that simple changes in ourselves can positively affect others.

Thank you for sharing our thoughts and beliefs.

K.K.

Where's Our Lamp?

Our deepest fear is not that we are inadequate. Our deepest fear is that we are powerful beyond measure. It is our light, not our darkness, that most frightens us. We ask ourselves, who am I to be brilliant, gorgeous, talented, fabulous? Actually, who are you not to be?

You are a child of God. Your playing small doesn't serve the world. There's nothing enlightened about shrinking so that other people won't feel insecure around you. We are all meant to shine, as children do. We were born to make manifest the glory of God that is within us. It's not just in some of us; it's in everyone. And as we let our own light shine, we unconsciously give other people permission to do the same. As we're liberated from our own fear, our presence automatically liberates others.

Marianne Williamson

A Handmaiden's Tale of an Illness

...disease is not something that a person 'has' and that is imposed upon him from the outside world; rather it is a failure of the 'total' individual to grow, function and adapt successfully to life's stresses.

Joan Luckmann and Karen Sorensen

I had the nice-nurse syndrome real bad! It oozed from my pores, messed with my mind and words — and not just at work but everywhere. I was sickly sweet. I was sick!

These were some of my symptoms:

- "Yes, right away, Doctor."
- "I'm sorry." (repeated ad nauseam)
- What did I do to upset him?
- "Yes, anything you say."
- No one ever thanks me.
- Nothing I do is ever good enough.

- Saying "yes, of course" when I want to say "no" and it would have been appropriate to say no.
- Not questioning a doctor's orders when I had questions.
- Smiling outwardly while being flaming mad inside.
- Anticipating the needs of others way too much.
- Making sure things were pleasant and controlled.
- Being aggressive, not assertive.
- "I don't mean to bother you."
- "What else can I do? What else can I do?"
- "If this isn't good enough, I can get such-and-such."
- "Here, let me help you," or "Here, I'll do that."

I was a crowd pleaser, an 'angel of mercy' with a tarnished halo, damaged wings, torn soul and battered heart. A savior of way too many. I was tired, oh so tired and very sad.

What was I doing wrong?

Where did this illness come from?

It came from my past years of conditioning in the 'mothering' art and my fears of not being liked, accepted and of being called selfish if I did not give, give, give!

The 'nice-nurse syndrome' was an insidious disease infecting my whole being, and I had allowed it to invade me.

I am flushing this syndrome from my system. All that extra water intake has helped immensely.

It still sneaks up and pops out at the oddest times. I feel it and see it coming on! I smile and laugh at myself and my silly disease. A lifetime of conditioning will take time to disappear.

It lays dormant, awaiting the day I eradicate the 'nice nurse syndrome' forever!

Multitasking Momma

For fast-acting relief, try slowing down.

Lily Tomlin

I have known, and still intimately know, a multi-tasking momma. She's a doer extraordinaire. A task master and a cousin to the 'nice nurse.' She astounds me with what she can do all at one time.

My goodness, she leaps tall buildings in a single bound while mowing the lawn, changing a diaper,

making a dentist's appointment, combing a child's hair and planning an entertaining dinner for 12. And as a nurse she is equally playing this role on her unit. She talks on the phone, fills out a requisition, is part way through some charting and at the same time or no question from her co-worker with a simple head nod. If the other phone rings, well, no problem, she can answer that one, too. She amazes me with this dual phone ability. All this I see from the outside — imagine what she has going on in her head!

I saw her in the mirror from time to time — she'd fly by in a flash — what I saw was super nurse. Bravado in a set of scrubs.

> You are enough. You have enough. You do enough.
>
> SARK

As time went along I saw less of a super nurse and more of a depleted one — her pace slowed and questions creased her brow.

"Why do I take all this on? Why am I doing it all? Why am I not happy?"

I could see she wanted answers. She wanted help and I gave it to her. I started learning to *be* and not to *do*.

There are three things that if a man does not know, he cannot live long in this world: what is too much for him, what is too little for him and what is just for him.

Swahili Proverb:

Dirty Little Secrets

Any sorrow can be borne if you can turn it into a story.
Isak Dinesen

Events often make heroes out of people, including care givers. I was addicted to the adrenalin rush of having a role in that drama. I needed to feel like I belonged with the group, wanting to be as smart, as fast, and as efficient as they seemed to be.

Stories of murder, mayhem and dismemberment were what I used to describe my work. They were my dirty little secrets, and telling them made me feel strong, intelligent and important — like a hero!

One very cold winter morning I was on shift in ER when we received a hypothermia victim. I called him Popsicle Man. This patient was frozen solid!

Honestly there was only one place on his body not rock hard.

I looked at the doctor and said, "You've got to be kidding me. This guy is way past our help."

"They're not dead until they are warm and dead," he replied

I tried to get a thermometer up his rectum with no success. His arm literally snapped off when I moved it to put on the blood pressure cuff.

I could not go on. I yelled for the doctor and after much debate he 'called the code.' Popsicle Man was officially dead.

What I carry around with me is that snapping sound. I close my eyes and can picture the scene as if it was yesterday, not 10 years ago. It nauseates me every time.

No one knew the depth of my feelings. I did not know how or understand why I needed to acknowledge them, if only to myself.

I used these stories to cover my feelings of inadequacy and lack of control. Heaven forbid that I would show any weaknesses. Until putting pen to paper I never admitted having feelings connected to the dirty little secrets.

These grotesque stories still come out now and then. First I look around to ensure non-medical people aren't listening. I've learned most 'normal' people cannot understand why we would think some of these things are funny and not horrible.

I think our dirty little secrets are horrible, but making jokes like "Now I have proof that a man's brains are in his penis," takes the focus off reality.

This black humor is a standard coping mechanism medical types have passed on from generation to generation. We stuff our true feelings down, find something to laugh at and then get back to work.

When mentoring younger nurses I often regaled them with these stories. Sometimes I set them up in order to get a laugh from their reactions. I helped to perpetuate this 'trial by fire'.

One evening in Emergency, the dispatch phone crackled away that paramedics were en route with an assault victim.

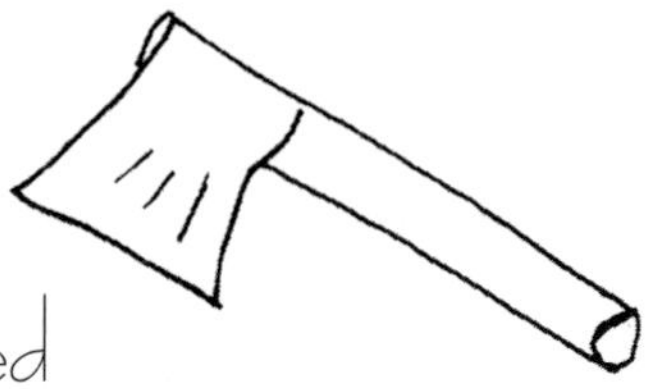

They were doing CPR on arrival and a hatchet was embedded in the unfortunate victim's head. I was orientating a young nurse who was nervous about working her first trauma. She had not yet seen the hatchet so I quickly got into her line of sight and instructed her to start with chest compressions. At just the 'right' time I called her name and stepped back. The look of shock and horror on her face gave me much delight and laughter.

I used this 'rite of passage' to show her how I dealt with the 'bad and the ugly' of our work. Creating opportunities for a laugh — a release — was all I knew how to do, all I'd been taught.

I hope she has been able to deal with the fallout from that initiation. She still works in Emergency and I know now that I did not mentor her properly. I never showed her how to deal with the emotions that come from our work.

I have mastered the technical skills. I am now honing the creation of an atmosphere that is conducive to my well being and also to the well-being of those around me.

> Talk not with judgment, greed, or envy but with compassion, wonder, and amazement.
>
> Unknown

Mushrooms

Remove price tags from people. Everyone has worth. The excitement lies in the discovery of their value.

Unknown

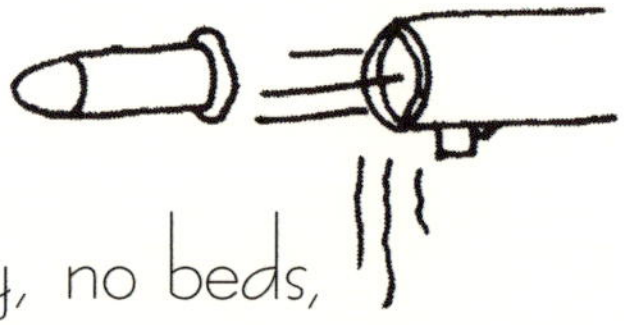

Outside influences streak in on me like bullets from a gun; no money, no beds, too many patients, hospital closures, privatization.

The worst part of this bombardment is that I receive no real information. No plan, no direction. I'm on the bottom of the need-to-know list and I feel like a mushroom in the manure pile, kept in the dark. The trouble is, I make up my own version of things, seeking tidbits from any source if I'm not supplied with information.

One day I was complaining to a colleague about the way the union over-bargains our contract.

"Did we need to ask for the whole loaf of bread when we just want a slice or two?"

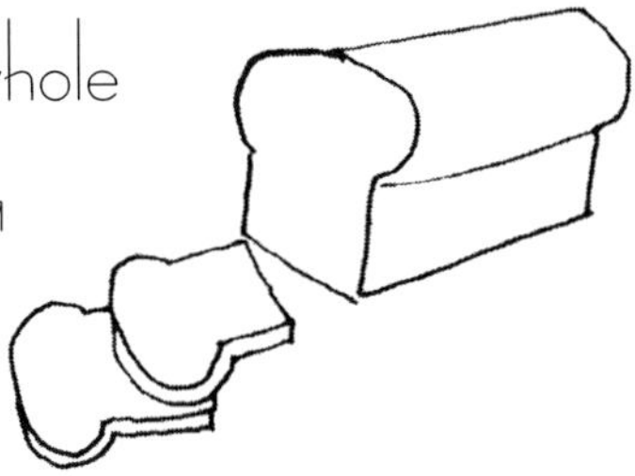

I felt greedy and ungrateful towards ourselves for wanting more. I had kept myself in the dark and needed some sun.

She listened to my tirade and calmly stated that if I really wanted to see some changes, I should come to a local union meeting and make it happen. Needing no other challenge, off I went. I came away having volunteered for a committee and from there I vaulted onto the local executive.

A valuable lesson was given to me that day. I had actually assumed some control over my work life. The more involved I became, the more satisfied I felt.

My need to manage the care of my patients and in my union role my need to care for fellow nurses, pushes me to be like a pit bull, relentless in figuring out the agenda and what the future is going to hold.

Having a working knowledge of the plans for the future fertilizes a sweet crop, not a field of weeds.

Keeper of the Keys

Don't make others problems your own. It only makes solving them twice as difficult.

Unknown

Carrying the burden of a heavy key chain is causing a hitch in my step. Not only am I hoisting around my patients but I carry around the responsibility for the rest of the health-care team.

Covering up for the doctors is my biggest burden. "What's taking him so long? Where are they? What's happening?"

"They're busy or maybe they're in their office. I'm sure they'll call as soon as they're able." I do this for them, not wanting the patient to lose faith or trust in their doctors and in the system.

I know full well that they're on the golf course or just plain not answering their calls.

Oh yeah, I took it all on. The Nobel peace prize should come my way!

Fellow co-workers would ask, "Could I have a taxi chit for my patient?"

"Why?" I responded.

"Well, it's a long way home. They live on the other side of town."

"If they walked here, they can walk home," I said, much to their dismay.

"How can you be so cold!" would be shot back at me.

Just walk through our doors, people. Line up and you now have anywhere from five to seven mothers. Come in with wet clothes and we'll give you dry ones. Have problems with your plumbing or your spouse? We'll try to keep you for as long as you need. Heaven forbid that we should remember that you have a brain or two feet. No problem, we'll carry your keys ,too.

Appease everyone.
Juggle all the keys. Oops!
Now I can't even find the
key for the med drawer.

I need an aspirin for my giant headache and sore hip.

If we continue to think like we've always thought, we'll continue to get what we've always got.

Jim Clemmer

The Drama Triangle

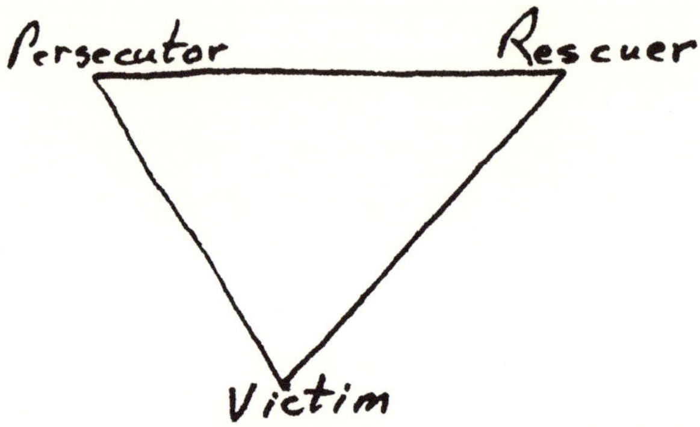

Stephen Karpman

When a colleague showed me the 'drama triangle' a few years ago, a light went on and there I was, looking at myself in a mirror.

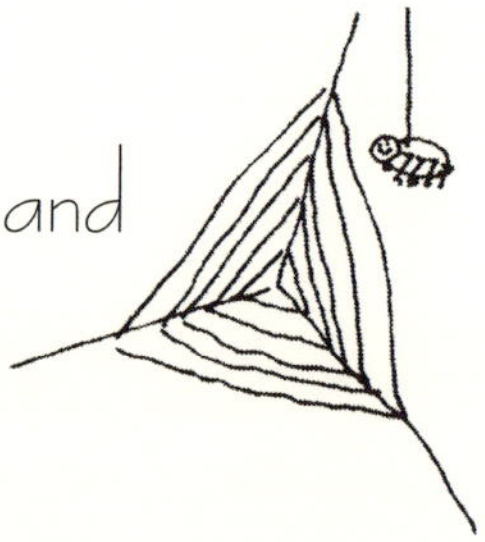

I was an A+ Rescuer, Persecutor and Victim. What a triangular web I had woven.

As a Rescuer, I possessed an "Oh, let me help you," mantra. I helped even when I didn't want to. And even when they did not want me to!

I was a 'smothering mother' and felt guilty if I didn't come to the rescue. I constantly strived to be the perfect nurse, mother and wife — the perfect Rescuer — but I was actually keeping others dependent upon me.

My heroics did not bring me what I wanted or needed, and I became angry. I found myself persecuting those very people I was so desperately trying to help. I blamed them for everything and was terribly critical. I shook my finger and screamed a lot. I trembled with anger.

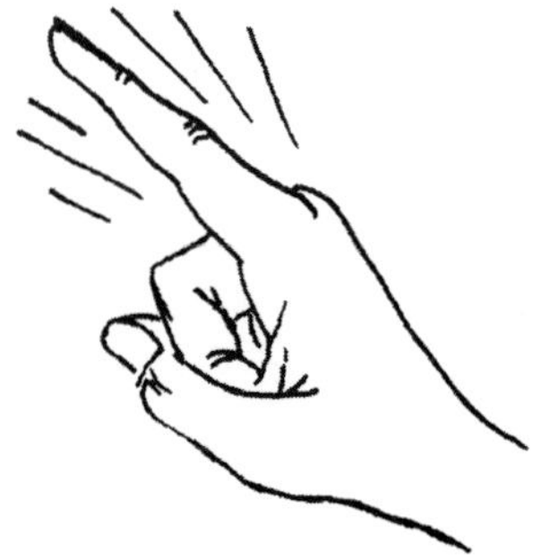

"Why can't they just do what I want?" I raged inwardly.

"It's all his fault."

"It's all your fault," but certainly not mine.

Good God, not mine!

I took none of the responsibility, yet felt I had it all and that NO ONE WAS HELPING!

I was sarcastic, and sarcasm became my forte. I could do battle with the best of them. Boy, could I do battle!

This anger frightened me. I did not want to

be nor stay angry, but I felt helpless to cope with it. This overwhelming feeling of despair spiraled downward into depression.

"Oh, why me? Why does this always happen to me?" No answer was forthcoming.

I was emotionally crushed and felt worthless. I gained 80 pounds. My self-confidence dwindled, and my self-esteem vanished. I wallowed in indecision and nothing could make me happy.

I realized that the harder I tried not to be a Persecutor, the better I was at being one of the other roles. From corner to corner on the triangle I went.

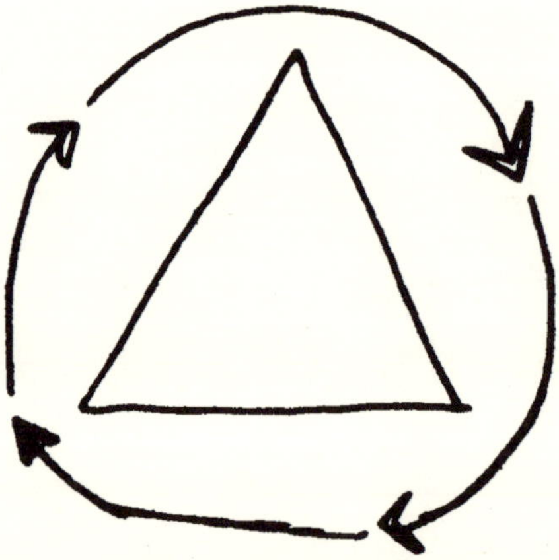

As I saw myself in every corner, a number of my behaviors suddenly made sense. It was the beginning of many endings, the beginning of many beginnings.

I realized my behaviors and my words were causing me pain. They were stopping me from meeting my needs.

Polishing Our Lamp

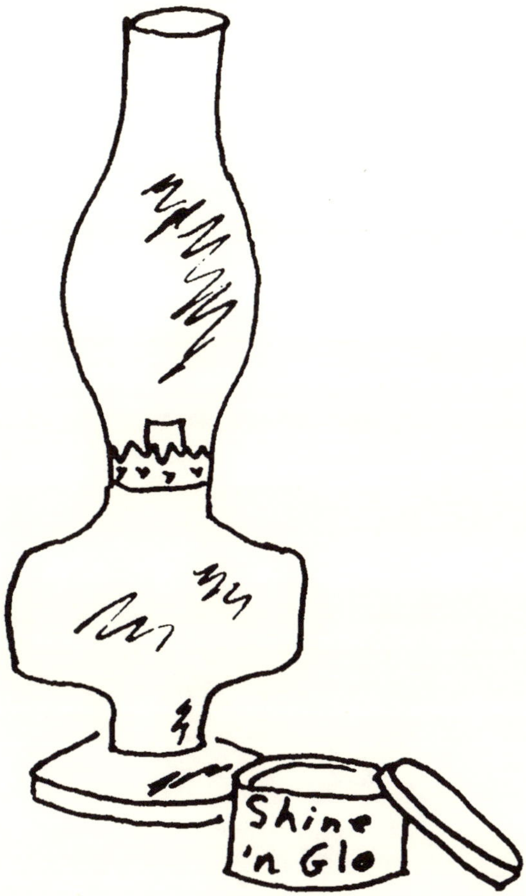

A Healthier Triangle

Have fun, be happy, and grow. Not to redeem, to prove, or to show.

Unknown

Developing healthier ways to feel, act and think allowed me to escape old triangular games.

I looked at those verbs and the letters F.A.T. emerged.

Gosh! I needed to get F.A.T. to become healthy. This was something I could relate to!

To become F.A.T., I chose to take responsibility for myself — responsibility for my feelings, my actions and my thoughts.

I moved away from the Rescuer role by allowing myself to experience and express my feelings. Placing my needs first and asking for what I need from others, continued this shift.

I am also giving up my expectations of other people and letting them be themselves. I no longer want to change or rescue people; becoming myself takes enough of my energy. I encourage others now, telling them I know they are capable people. Rather than thinking for others by guessing what they need or want, I now ask them what their needs are.

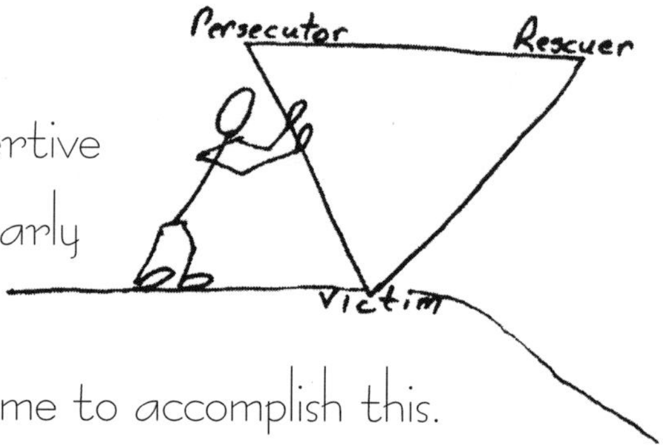

I moved from being a Persecutor to being assertive and genuine. Thinking clearly and being honest with myself and others helped me to accomplish this. I no longer say things to make others feel good or because I think it is what they want me to say.

Now, I say what I mean and mean what I say. Instead of blaming others, I take responsibility for my own problems. When and if I need help, I ask for it. I do not attempt to do everything or solve every problem alone.

I moved out of the Victim role by taking action and staying determined not to be defeated. I acted, knowing there was always something to do — there was always an answer.

Taking these responsibilities is about telling my truths, as boldly yet lovingly as possible, to myself as well as others.

These responsibilities are about making choices and then mustering the courage to follow through with them.

Some people — who are still very much imprisoned on the triangle — don't like my changes.

"What's happening to you? What do you mean, 'no'? You're being cruel," are typical responses.

I have weathered complaints of selfishness, not being caring, abandoning my responsibilities as a mother and friend, and even of being crazy.

Whenever I step away from my old games, people around me may see me in a Persecutor role. As I say "no", ask for what I need and work to have my needs met, others sometimes see this as being aggressively assertive and certainly unbecoming! To them, this is not WHO Kathy is/was. Achieving this honesty, to myself and others, has been a painful process. At times I felt as if folks I was now being truly honest with were throwing daggers at my back. I have shed many tears as I left my old behaviors behind, but I am using healthier ones now.

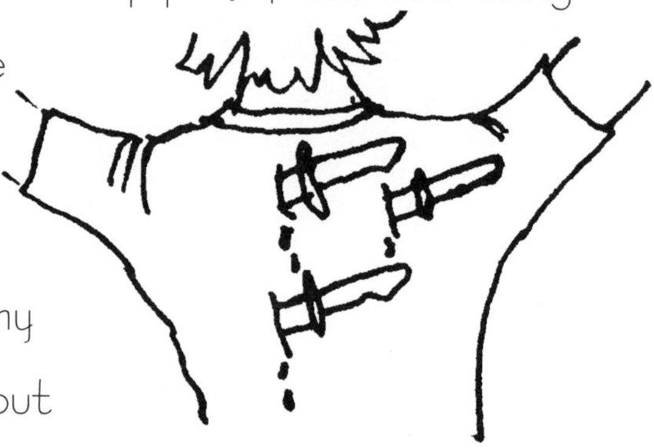

I was recently told that I am 'honest to a fault'. I smiled and took it as a compliment! I am proud to be considered to be this honest. I will continue to summon the courage to be honest with myself and others, providing clear and direct communication.

Am I still imprisoned within the triangle at times? You bet!

Those angles were my whole being until a few years ago, and it will take a lifetime of effort before I can finally leave them behind. Slowly but surely, I am becoming a healthier, more authentic me.

And those 80 pounds I gained while wallowing in victimhood? Fifty have left me. I believe this is happening because I am becoming true to myself.

If nothing ever changed, there would be no butterflies.

Unknown

Autobiography in Five Short Chapters

Chapter 1

I walk down the street
There's a deep hole in the sidewalk.
And I fall in.
I'm lost. I'm helpless.
It takes forever to find a way out.

Chapter 2

I walk down the same street
There's a deep hole in the sidewalk.
I pretend I don't see it and I fall in
again.
I can't believe I'm in the same place,
But it isn't my fault.
It still takes a long time to get out.

Chapter 3

I walk down the same street.

There's a deep hole in the sidewalk.
I see it is there, I still fall in
because it's a habit.
But my eyes are open and I know
where I am.
It is my fault and I get out
immediately.

Chapter 4

I walk down the same street.
There's a deep hole in the sidewalk.
I walk around it.

Chapter 5

I walk down a different street.

from *There's a hole in my Sidewalk*, by Portia Nelson

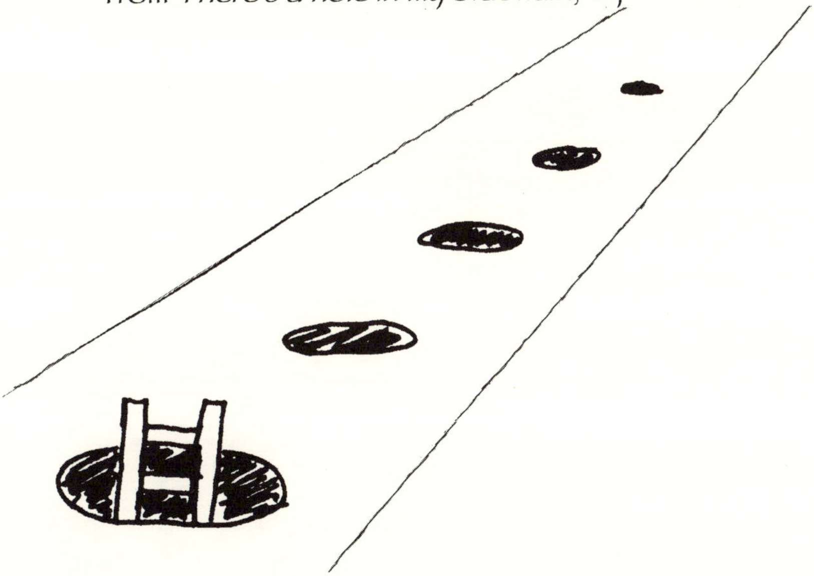

I walk down a different street in many areas of my life. I've reached Chapter 4 for some but only Chapter 3 for others! I laugh at myself as I see the holes and the triangle positions that hook me. When I fall in I carry my Mickey Mouse flashlight to light my way out.

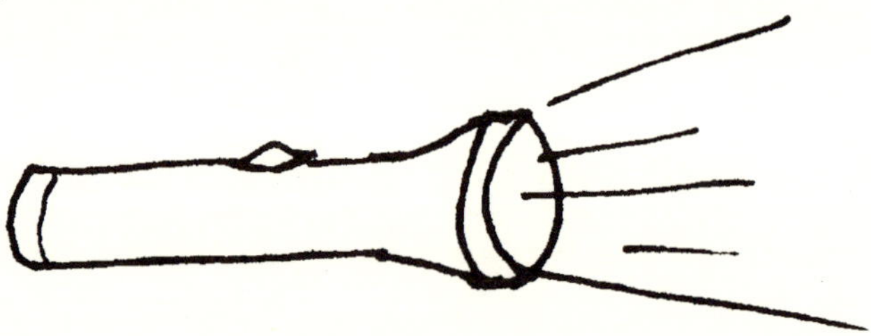

Mirror, Mirror

Deep into that darkness peering, long I stood there, wondering, fearing, doubting, dreaming dreams no mortal ever dared to dream before.

Edgar Allan Poe

I want to hear nurses identify themselves in a way that clearly describes who they are. "I'm a nurse," is not enough. It's like saying, "I'm a woman."

I had never faced my identity, until I struggled with 'what if?'

What if I can't continue to work as a nurse?

I know I am not alone, I've had others confide these same fears to me.

Am I only the job?

Is it so inseparably tied to my person? Who am I, if

not a nurse?

I boldly stepped up to the mirror and learned a new way of seeing myself and of describing who I am.

I, Linda Bridge, am a woman and a nurse. And so much more.

I am a golfer and an avid reader. I am smart, funny, an auntie supreme, a sister, a daughter and a friend.

I am, as all other nurses intelligent, courageous, heroic, efficient, adaptable, strong, respected, inventive, privileged and creative.

I am an advocate and a social activist.

Courage, sacrifice, determination, commitment, toughness, heart, talent, guts. That's what girls are made of; the hell with sugar and spice.

Unknown

I love my role as a nurse. I am proud of my accomplishments and plan to continue for as long as my body can cope with the demands placed on it by my profession.

I know of no other group of people who put on clean clothes and a smile and go into a work place full of deadly bugs, violent patients and not enough staff.

Trudy Richardson (friend and teacher)

I have had to change departments, learn new skills, and decrease my working hours. I remain productive and enjoy myself. If I had to quit, I have no doubt I would find other work.

Intelligent as I am, I could not grasp that concept until I was forced to look deeper at my strengths and weaknesses.

You are the perfect you! You have something to offer that will never again be possible. To devalue this is not only a tragedy for you but, in fact, the world.

Unknown

I know my outer persona does not match how I often perceive myself. My friends and colleagues would scoff at me, declaring that I am timid and shy at times.

I concentrate on my strengths, telling myself things like I am 'quantitatively qualified', not 'credentially challenged'.

I am a bloom fertilizer (you figure that one out!), master intravenous inserter, a conflict diffuser, a shoulder to lean on, and a pair of ears (one good one anyway) that know how to listen.

Most of all I am content with who I am and excited about where I am going. Do I ever have periods of self doubt? You bet!

Do I linger with those thoughts? No way! I use them to measure how I feel about what I am doing, where I am going and how I'm living on the way.

Our limitations, our imperfections, our mistakes... these do not reflect our inferiority, but are part of being human.

Joan Sheingold Ditzion

The Guy in the Glass

When you get what you want in your struggle for pelf,
And the world makes you King for a day,
Then go to the mirror and look at yourself,
And see what that guy has to say.
For it isn't your Father, or Mother, or Wife,
Who judgement upon you must pass.
The feller whose verdict counts most in your life
Is the guy staring back from the glass.
He's the feller to please, never mind all the rest,
For he's with you clear up to the end,
And you've passed your most dangerous, difficult test
If the guy in the glass is your friend.
You may be like Jack Horner and "chisel" a plum,
And think you're a wonderful guy,
But the man in the glass says you're only a bum

If you can't look him straight in the eye.
You can fool the whole world down the pathway of years,
And get pats on the back as you pass,
But your final reward will be heartaches and tears
If you've cheated the guy in the glass.

by Dale Wimbrow, ©1934

Nightingale News

I have but one lamp by which my feet are guided, and that is the lamp of experience. I know of no way of judging the future but by the past.

Unknown

I do not recall learning a great deal about Florence Nightingale in nursing school. She was just there, around me. . . a presence. It was as if the very mention of her name was a sanctity within the hallowed halls of a hospital.

And, gosh, for me back then, it was! I thought of her as 'the lady with the lamp,' nurse of all nurses. The angelic guru of our profession.

Throughout my career her name popped up, often with not quite the same reverence as earlier. But you know, I never really understood what she was all about.

She gave nursing a public standing and independence within the medical hierarchy that it would otherwise have taken much longer to consolidate. Her emphasis on common sense care was invaluable and she greatly strengthened the vocational aura of nursing by her posturing, but she added nothing to the details of technical proficiency required in a nurse's daily tasks.

F.B. Smith

Learning more about Miss Nightingale led me to develop a whole other impression of this woman. I believe she was a lady, not only with a flickering lamp, but with a flaming self-respect which outshone most women of her time. She had values and visions for nursing that spoke of art, fortitude and leadership. Florence Nightingale was a far cry from the whispery "yes, doctor" handmaiden I had previously envisioned.

Nursing is an art; and if it to be made an art, it requires as exclusive a devotion, as hard a preparation, as any painter's or sculptor's work. It is one of the Fine Arts; I had almost said the finest of the Fine Arts.

Florence Nightingale

I saw and felt sparks of Florence glowing within me.

But I wanted to feel the bright, bursting flames of her spirit, so I undertook the overhauling of my lamp.

I set out to honor the artist within me, to pay homage to my past assertions and strengths as a woman and a nurse. I am uncovering my most true self.

The movie 'Shrek' comes to mind as I write this.

Would Florence have enjoyed this ogre? Totally!

I believe that, as with Shrek, she had peeled her onion layers well back to unmask all of herself. She was truly and deeply her own person.

Shrek worked on his layers and I am working on mine, to become oh so much more of a "succulent pungent bulb" (a dictionary definition) and to find and expose my core!

I am celebrating my creativity in light of my new perspective of nursing as an art. I will no longer allow it to be squelched.

Over the last 25 years I have connected with countless nurses, and among them are some of the most creative souls I have ever met. These artists are the most profound out-of-the-box thinkers I know!

I am proud to be a nurse in the image of Florence. I will continue to polish my lamp, and I invite you to embark upon this creative voyage.

It is not because things are difficult that we do not dare;
it is because we do not dare that they are difficult.

Seneca

Credential Creations

Reasonable people adapt themselves to the world. Unreasonable people attempt to adapt the world to themselves. All progress, therefore, depends on unreasonable people.

George Bernard Shaw

When we became serious about writing this book, a friend of ours in the know asked a telling question; "What kind of credentials do you have?"

"You mean we need more than 50 years of combined beside nursing?"

"Oh," was his reply. He went on to suggest that possibly we needed someone with academic credentials to support our project by adding an element of professional credibility.

We explained we did not need a Ph.D., Master's, or even a Bachelor's degree to write a nursing book. We needed the courage and tenacity to uncover the colossal credentials we already possessed within us.

This was not for the faint-hearted. Telling tales of lamp overhauls takes guts and stamina.

Our friend was listening now.

We demonstrated our worth and value by accentuating our positives and negating our negatives. We ultimately gained the auspicious title of *hopelessly human* nurses.

Here are our credentials:

Linda Bridge: RN, CC, GG, AA, CC, SA, CI, OH, TD, FO, TKT, AA, SS, HHN, Etc.

Registered Nurse, Cheerleading Champ, Gloriously Graceful, Abundantly Able, Creative Clown, Social Activist, Caring Individual, Overly Honest, Driven , Family Oriented, Traveling Karaoke Troubadour, Aquatic Angel, Smashing Smiler, *hopelessly human* Nurse, Etc. And I have black leather curtains in my bedroom.

Kathy Knowles: RN, SS, BE, SA, GF, TH, PL, CE, PIP, HHN, PB, CS, Etc.

Registered Nurse, Smile Specialist, Baker Extraordinaire, Stone Aficionado, Generous Friend, Tree Hugger, Passionate Lover, Communication Expert, Perfectly Imperfect, *hopelessly human* Nurse, Process Believer, Courageous Soul, Etc. And I do not have black leather curtains in my bedroom!

Wishin' Permission

With courage you will dare to take risks, have the strength to be compassionate and the wisdom to be humble. Courage is the foundation of integrity.

Keshavan Nair

Inbred within me was a need for 'permission.' In childhood I required permission from my parents to do anything and everything. I even felt that sense of needing permission when I attended the Grace General Hospital School of Nursing. I lived in residence and had housemothers to check on me, not parents.

Living on my own for five years started me on the road to freedom from my collar and leash. I was growing assertively as a young nurse at the same time.

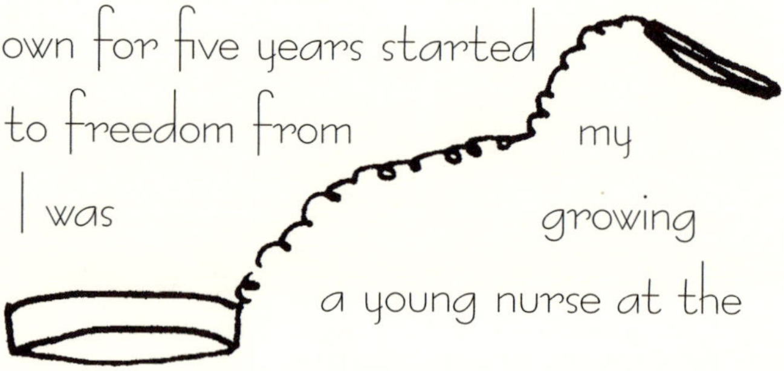

I allowed this need for permission back into my life when I married. I felt caught again and I struggled with this for a very long time.

I knew that permission for myself didn't come from someone else, yet I was steeped in the old feeling of needing it.

No one had authority over me and I knew I needed to take back the reins of my self-determination. This meant permission to care for myself first, to feel my feelings, to cry, to laugh with exuberance, to do less, to 'be' more and to just be ME!

> Kathy, I hereby grant you permission to be you.
>
> Signed,
>
> Kathy Knowles RN, etc.

I wish for all other nurses the permission to be themselves, and to own their own authority.

If you cannot learn to act without masters, you evidently will never become the real equal of those who do.

Dr. Mary Putnam Jacobi (1864)

Unselfishly Selfish

We have a responsibility to treat ourselves kindly; then we will treat the world in the same way.

Natalie Goldberg

I prided myself on being one of the most unselfish people on Earth. I practically gave myself away.

Something wasn't right as my thoughts left me with sentences such as... "If I keep giving myself away, who gives to me? When is it my turn? Is this all there is? I feel so run down and empty."

I read self-help books but the words seemed so selfish to me. I was quick to put them down, to dismiss them for their hedonism. I read the messages but never absorbed their full meaning.

I mulled over selfishness while I continued

giving myself away, and still feeling that I was missing something big.

During an anxious early-morning phone call several years ago, my brother gave me advice that heralded a healthy connection to selfishness.

"Kathy," he said, "put your oxygen mask on first before making any decisions or helping anyone else."

There I was in the front entry of my home, visualizing myself shakily pulling an oxygen mask over my terrified face. I had always thought those instructions were for crashing 747's, not for on-earth survival.

My brother's words aided me through a life crisis that day. I have made them a part of my everyday living. They led me to the 'something big' that was missing: *me!*

I am a healthy selfish person. If someone says to me, "but that's selfish," I tell them to sell the 'fishy' part of the word. And, voila. Selfish is no longer stinky.

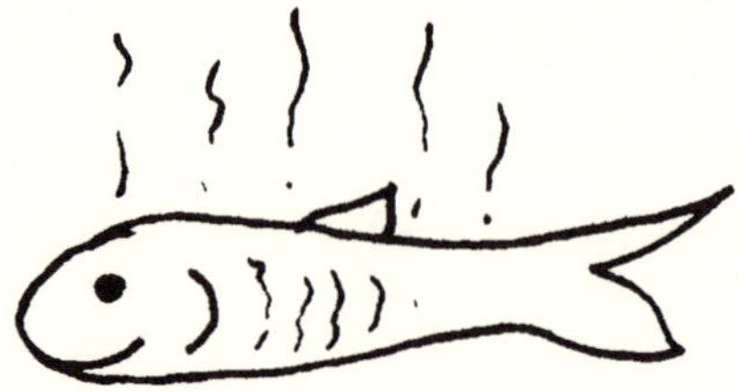

The mask scene is with me as I write these words and serves as a vivid reminder to look after myself first. This healthy selfish act is paramount for the wellbeing of those who depend on me. And I depend on me more than anyone else does!

Hopelessly Human

by Linda Bridge

Are you hopelessly human?
I try hard not to be
I am a nurse, you see!

I thought it was something
I ought not to be
I am a nurse, you see!

Fresh, young, new shoes
New job, a chance to be free
I am a nurse, you see!

A few years later
It's too hard to be me
I am a nurse, you see!

I'm hopelessly human
Now I realize I need to be
I am a nurse, you see!

Overhaul Warning

Guilt: the gift that keeps on giving.

Erma Brombeck

I stood with my reflection for some time before I selfishly prepared to celebrate my new-found credentials.

Once I'd cavorted with Shrek and Florence, I grabbed my permission slip and bravely set off to overhaul my lamp.

My steps were strong. I was charged! Yet my gut felt funny. I couldn't name what was wrong. And as I reached for my wick. . . WHAM!

"What if peoples' feelings are hurt as I change and grow? Am I doing something wrong? Will I be offensive? Is any of this criminal?"

As I heard it, I named it: Guilt

I was allowing it to paralyze me before I even got out of the starting gate. I was not going to let this happen. I had been readying myself for a long while, and I was not going to stay put!

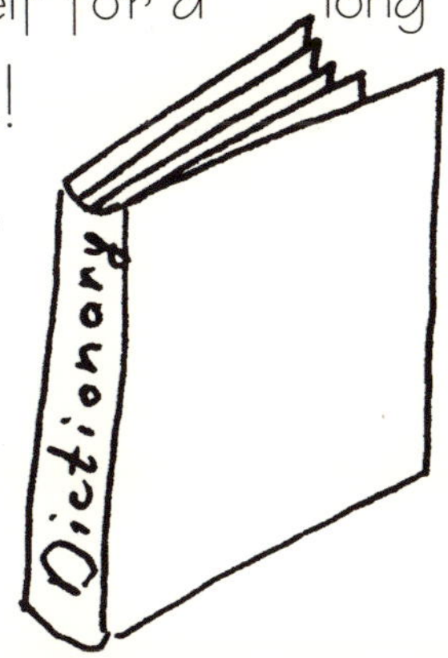

I took my dictionary and flipped to 'G'. Reading the definition of 'guilt' helped me put things into perspective.

I was not planning to commit an offense, crime or violation. I did not need to feel responsible or remorseful for other people's feelings.

My morals were intact. These were my feelings, actions and thinking I was changing.

Doing this is not a criminal act.

This is my lamp, my life. No court of law is present to condemn me for becoming a healthier me. I will not be pulled before a judge and jury to hear the gavel slam down a guilty

verdict.

I was not going to sit in self-judgment and I rendered guilt powerless.

I began to laugh at my gut reactions and now there is nary a twinge.

Warning heard! Case closed!

When I was young and free and my imagination had no limits, I dreamed of changing the world.

As I grew older and wiser, I discovered the world would not change, so I shortened my sights somewhat and decided to change only my country. But it too seemed immovable.

As I grew into my twilight years, in one last desperate attempt, I settled for changing only my family, those closest to me, but alas, they would have none of it.

And now as I lie on my deathbed, I suddenly realize: If I had only changed myself first, then by example I might have changed my family.

From their inspiration and encouragement, I would then have been able to better my country, and, who knows, I may have even changed the world.

Unknown

Our New Wick

Teeter-totter Tactics

Hear and you forget; See and you remember; Do and you understand.

Confucius

I remember enthusiastically running for one end of the teeter-totter as my sister ran for the other. Me being a chubby young miss and her being a skinny-minny. . . well, you get the picture. I quickly lost my enthusiasm.

At first, I left the responsibility for a safe and pleasant journey to the kids on the other end. When this didn't work I tried yelling at them, barking instructions, and crying if I didn't get what I wanted. I pouted, pleaded and often walked away in a huff.

"Move forward."

"Move back."

"Get Jim to sit with you — no, no, not Henry, too."

And with Henry came my initiation into the world of catapulting.

I was not the child wanting to feel the exhilaration of being airborne, nor do I possess this burning desire

as an adult. Possibly that is why I did not take up figure skating.

If my ride wasn't fun, I blamed the others. I hated their tricks, yet I also played them.

I soon experimented with doing things at my end of the board. Moving up, moving back, adding one friend, and then another. I realized I could be accountable for my own gleeful pleasure.

I also stopped playing tricks, and soon a different set of kids was attracted to teeter with me. I became choosy. But despite my changes, I still walked away on occasion.

Time and tactics prevailed to balance and ride the seemingly impossible length of 2x12 plank.

As a kid, I was playing in the playground. As an adult, with the little girl still very much inside of me, I am playing in the playground of life.

It was an 'ah ha' moment for me when I first realized the parallels. Somewhere over the past 40-plus years I had forgotten I had choices. I could change!

Teeter-totter savvy continues to serve me well as a nurse.

Within me lies the solution to being neither catapulted to Cleveland nor destined to fall flat on my butt.

The challenge is to enjoy my ride.

I am learning to be in control of myself on the teeter-totter and not to attempt to control others. And I no longer attempt to manipulate the plank !

The solutions lie within me. I have choices.

Due to circumstances beyond my control, I am master of my fate and captain of my soul.

Ashleigh Brilliant

I Stand on Par with Thee

No one can make you feel inferior without your consent.

Eleanor Roosevelt

I believe physicians are like every other Tom, Dick and Harry, Mary, Margaret and Sue: human beings deserving of equal respect.

I used to, and at times still do, elevate them above their humanness.

I called them Doctor.

I was told to do this from a very early age and it was further ingrained during my nurse's training. In my mind they held a status akin to God and I felt inferior to this authority.

In my younger days I worked in an Intensive Care Unit with six beds. The layout was cramped and not conducive to crowds of workers. On one of those crowed days I was dealing with a post-operative patient, and there were three specialists standing at the foot of the bed. I was kneeling on the floor emptying an overflowing catheter bag. Being the organized whiz kid, I filled up two buckets, to the brim!

All was fine until I tried to get up. That impressive stethoscope clipped around my neck had somehow managed to hook itself on the hem of my uniform skirt. There I was with two very full buckets of pee, and every time I tried to stand, up lifted my dress. I felt like a peep show in front of three physicians!

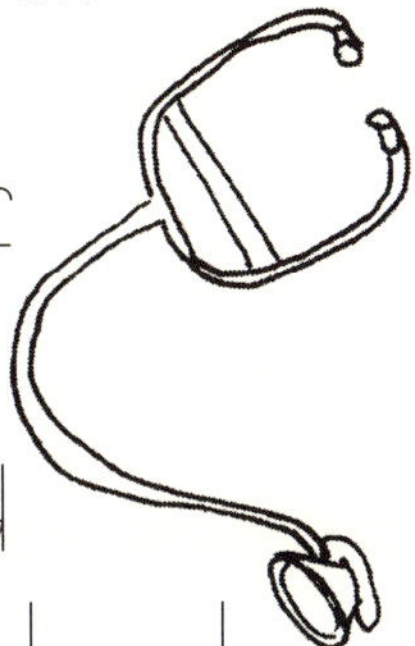

What was I going to do? If I put down the buckets inevitably some would spill. If I stood up to go and empty them, I would continue to expose myself to three VIPs. How would I ever show my face to them again without blushing?

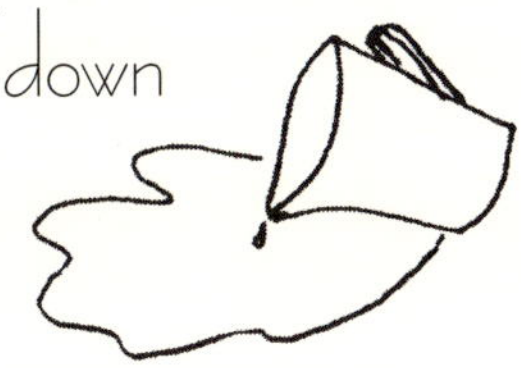

At last, one of the more gentlemanly of the three giggling doctors said to his colleague closest to me, "Blair, shouldn't you unhook her?"

"No way. This is too much fun," he replied.

I shot them a scathing look and set the buckets down, miraculously spilling only a drop or two.

Those three doctors fell off their pedestals that day, allowing me to see them as human. They were more like my brothers than those unreachable men who wielded the title 'Doctor.'

Once I saw physicians as hopelessly human, just like myself, I simply changed my choice of designation. This has made a world of difference. First-name-basis is standard practice for me now.

I had unwittingly placed myself in an inferior position, and I have chosen not to stay there. This choice was mine and mine alone to make.

Feelings of inferiority and superiority are the same. They both come from fear.

Robert Anthony

There are a select number of physicians whom I refer to as Doctor, this being a sign of respect for senior age more than anything else.

Other physicians will be called Doctor by me

from time to time, but usually out of a laziness on my part to learn their first names. And if I think about it, that in itself is disrespectful.

I also use the Doctor title when I am jokingly talking with one.

"Hello, Ms. Knowles." "Good day to you, Dr. Jones." Both of us are speaking in 'that' voice!

If a physician asked me not to call him or her by their first name, I would take their request into consideration. The final choice would be mine. My own self-respect comes first, and I would always bring myself back to this point in my decision making.

If a physician asked me to call him Doctor in front of patients, again I would take this into consideration, knowing I had the final choice.

I see patients as being in partnership with the health-care team. I want them to feel they're on equal footing on this team, allowing them the freedom to ask questions and voice their needs.

This ideal is not what I usually see; a somewhat inferior placement of the patient exists in the minds of many. (This inferiority may be patient-, nurse- or doctor-driven.)

If calling doctors by their first names helps the patients, I will do it. I choose to support the most vulnerable of the team, and I see this person as being the patient.

I believe these choices bring everyone on par, allowing a healthier system to emerge out of mutual self-respect.

Value yourself — the only people who appreciate a doormat are people with dirty shoes.

Unknown

Returning the Keys

A healthy source of support cares about our pain but does not carry it for us or try to cure it.

Unknown

I once mistakenly believed I was totally responsible for my patients. I've now learned to ask myself, "Are they competent?"

If the answer is yes, then they are capable of making their own decisions, which includes living at risk. My obligation to patients is to provide them with the knowledge and information needed to make healthy choices.

As a hospital supervisor, I once received a call from a nurse asking me how to find the social worker on call. Of course, I asked why. They had a patient who had been a victim of family violence. The doctor had left an order for her to go to a woman's shelter.

I asked the nurse if she had talked with the patient herself? And was the patient willing to go to a shelter?

The nurse sounded surprised, responding that the doctor had talked with the patient.

I knew, having worked in Emergency for 18 years, that battered women will often say anything just to get you to go away.

By the time I reached the unit, the nurse told me the patient had no intention of going to a shelter and had instead made plans to go to her sister's home. I made sure the patient had all the necessary phone numbers and contact names that she might find useful in the future. It was her choice to use them or not.

At one time I had been overwhelmed and frustrated about being responsible for everyone's every need. I had rescued patients, not respected their choices.

When I started treating my patients more as partners in their own health care, they began responding in the way I'd hoped. As I showed respect to patients, they in turn respected me.

What a feeling of relief it is not to carry everyone's life as my personal responsibility.

Feel WITH other people, not FOR them.

I had the honor of witnessing a transition from 'keeper of the keys' to 'returning the keys' with the care of a young, morbidly obese patient. She had been hospitalized on numerous occasions, and each time no unit wanted to care for her. There was always the problem of providing a properly sized bed; at one time two beds were bolted together before a specially designed bed was rented for the admission of such large patients.

Inevitably, numerous behavioral issues surfaced in

both the patient and the staff.

The situation regressed into a tug-of-war with neither side winning. Tempers flared and health problems did not improve for this bed-ridden patient. At one point she nearly died, and on another occasion she was being processed for long-term care placement. The staff's health was steadily worsening as well.

Then a new physiotherapist arrived on the unit to care for the patient. He sparked a completely new perspective of this woman as a human being. He started to give her back her responsibility by giving her choices and encouragement.

A turning point occurred during discharge planning rounds when the unit's charge nurse had an 'ah ha' moment.

"You mean WE have been contributing to this lady's behavior?" the nurse asked. "We're just as at fault as she is? Oh, oh! I get it now. Look at what we've done."

Her next question was how this unhappy state of affairs could be changed, and ideas were offered by those present.

The patient slowly and steadily healed. She lost weight and began to walk again with the aid of a walker. Many weeks later, she was discharged to her own home.

A dramatic final moment came several months later when this lady arrived to visit an ailing relative. Staff lined the halls and cheered as she walked around the corner into the unit. Smiles beamed and tears glistened, as if to light her path.

I saw that her smile was the widest of all. I believe the entire health-care team cared enough to give this patient back her keys, and in return she helped them become hopelessly human.

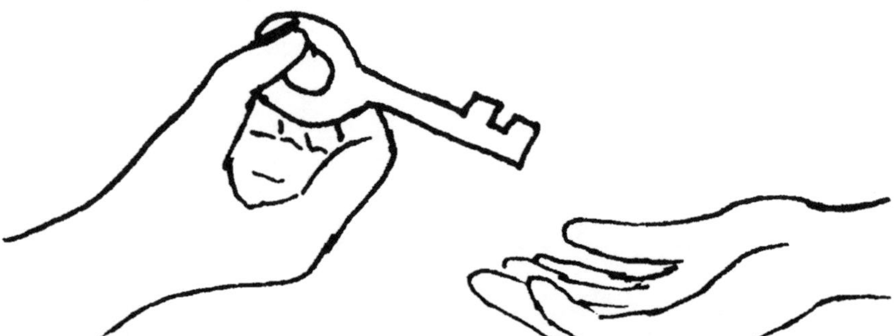

To Be or Not To Be

Nothing we do is ever as important as how we be.

Unknown

It was never a question of 'doing' for me. I was and can still be a very successful doer! When it came to 'being' though, I hadn't the foggiest clue how to accomplish that. 'Being' was unheard of in my world until I became ill in the early 1990s.

Yes, at first I fought it. I wouldn't even admit I was sick, let alone seek help. "Who, me? I'm just a bit tired. Maybe if I sleep more and stop working full 18-hour days."

I tried.

I would not accept illness into my world. No bloody way! I blamed everything and everyone, including myself.

Then came a day when my fever spiked

to 41° Celsius and I could not get out of bed. I had barely been able to climb stairs before the fever, and now not at all. There I was, stuck, my mind still doing, doing, doing while my body was on vacation in the Sahara.

I had no choice but to 'be', and I painfully learned to let go of 'doing' — very painfully.

I was questioned about the validity of my illness, my sanity, my acceptance of even higher piles of dishes and even dirtier floors.

I questioned these things too and I was scared to death. Scared I would never 'do' again!

I half-heartedly gave myself permission to sit still. As I learned to 'be', the 'to-do' lists shrunk. In my mind, though, I was secretly plotting to start full-steam ahead as soon as I could 'go' again. This thinking caught up with me too.

I could not secretly 'do' anything without my mind knowing about it. Darn it all, anyway. It was telling me LOUD AND CLEAR to just BE!!

I sat for long hours watching the world through the picture window in my kitchen. From my rocker by the wood stove I viewed scenes of nature in the moment. The sun playing on the snow, a fox sneaking past Fanny, our dog, and a snowy owl perched atop a pole watching for lunch to appear in the field. Those moments were crucial to my health.

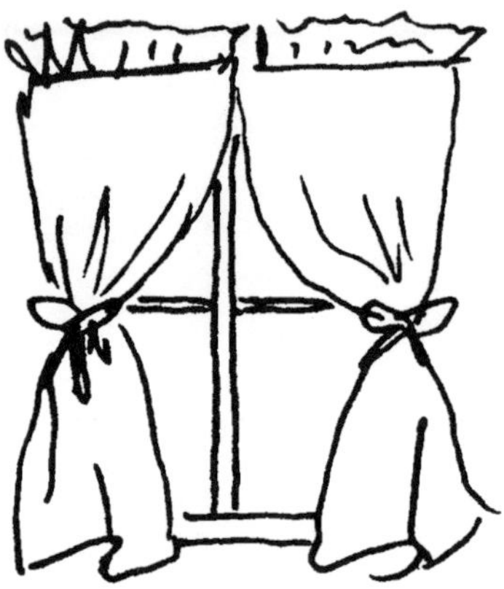

When I sat, I sat; when I walked, I walked. I did not take up knitting and 'do' that too. Nor did I pick up garbage in the yard or pull a few weeds along my path. 'Moment by moment,' was what I taught myself.

It seemed so simple but was soooo hard.

I see 'being' as an art; 'doing' as a science.

'Being.' I will never master, but I will practice it.

'Doing,. I will never let master me again.

I work at balancing.

Do be do be do"

Frank Sinatra

And stay away from the unhealthy.

Do do do do Do do do do

Beethoven

Feeling the Feelings

We often despise what is most useful to us.

Aesop

Mad, Sad, Glad and Fear are the four true feelings. I was scared to feel them.

As feelings rose in me, I hid them, squelched them, and shoved them down deep, to deal with another time. Another time never came.

I conditioned myself to do this after being castigated for slamming doors, laughing loudly, screaming, crying and voicing my anxieties. As I expressed these I was cut down, shut

down, put down, teased, stopped and judged.

"Don't laugh so loud."

"Don't act like that."

"Don't cry."

"Don't feel that way."

"You shouldn't get angry."

"Don't get too close."

"Don't be so distant."

I allowed others to effectively disrespect, disapprove and direct me in how I needed to feel! I let unhealthy fears rule, which left me empty, void, numb. . . dead.

I allowed myself to become an anesthetized zombie, an angel of mercy turned to stone. Even sicker, I kept apologizing for my actions — apologizing for being human.

As I overhaul my lamp, I allow myself to feel Mad, Sad and Glad. And I am putting Fear into perspective.

Deadly Fear

Fear is that little darkroom where negatives are developed.

Michael Pritchard

Fears have always controlled me. I allowed them to run my life. I am working to define my imagined fears and my real ones.

The true terror of feeling that my life, in this instant, is going to be taken from me, is my 'real' fear!

I have faced this moment at least a half-dozen times.

As I compare that horror to the fear of quitting my job, dating, giving a speech or flying to Europe, the latter ones aren't fears. They are anxieties.

Having put these into perspective, I now work at keeping them separate and dealing with them in a whole different light. As I accept being hopelessly human, I lessen my anxieties.

Sad: Crying is No Laughing Matter

It is only the women whose eyes have been washed clear with tears who get the broad vision that makes them little sisters to all the world.

Dorothy Dix

I was not taught — or allowed — to cry.

"Stop crying!" "Now what are you crying about?" "Big girls don't cry." "You're just being emotional... Is it 'that time' of the month?" These shaped why I viewed the flow of tears as a sign of weakness.

And good God, I must not be weak!

Even when my son was critically ill at birth, I was discouraged from crying by the one person I thought would let me show it: my older sister who is a nurse.

I felt I should never be sad or feel anything. So, over many years I sucked sadness up and stuffed sadness down.

Death after traumatic death in my emergency nursing career never fazed me. Very few tears escaped these eyes in the presence of others, or even when I was alone.

"I must not cry, I must not cry," was the voice in my head.

And, God forbid, if any tears should sneak out in front of anyone, I immediately apologized for my actions. I realize now I was apologizing for being human!

I prided myself on being stoic. But silently growing in me was apathy and a dead zone.

I wanted to cry. I longed to cry, especially in a safe environment of support. I no longer wanted tears to spill out guiltily on my drives home from work or in front of my young son at a totally unrelated moment.

As I polished my lamp, I looked at crying... and at feeling.

I was terrified to cry. I feared if I started I would

never stop. I have had others, men and women, voice this same concern.

Eventually, I gave myself permission and let myself cry and cry and cry and cry and cry and cry.

An 18-wheeler-load of Kleenex has driven through my home over the last five years. My trash can runneth over with my past sorrows. I tied the bags and threw away all the old garbage.

I believe my 'weeping and wailing' saved my life. I began to feel again, see again, begin again and be human. I found food tasted better, smells became sharper, colors brighter. And I felt alive.

I released a great deal of 'stuff' I'd shoved down deep inside to forget, deal with another day, deny, gloss over and endure.

Tears carry creative power... In fairy tales, tears change people, remind them of what is important and save their souls... tears call things to us, they correct things, provide the missing part or piece... Tears not only represent feeling but are also lenses through which we gain an alternative vision, another point of view.

Clarissa Pinkola Estes

I no longer want to be around people who tell me not to cry. I am on the hunt for red-eye admirers who will just sit with me when I bawl.

An onion can make people cry, but there has never been a vegetable invented to make them laugh.

Will Rogers

Glad: Jiggle, Wiggle, and Giggle

Dogs laugh, but they laugh with their tails. What puts man in a higher state of evolution is that he has got his laugh on the right end.

Max Eastman

Humor, when wisely used, lifts my spirits as nothing else. I say "wisely" because if done at the expense of someone else, it becomes a source of conflict or hurt. Being sensitive to the type of practical jokes I played on co-workers was something I learned over time.

Fortunately for me, I worked alongside a professional practical joker. This nurse had an arsenal of fake poop and vomit, and an imagination for putting inflated latex gloves into places that I won't go into.

Fake patients were a mainstay of

humour as well, catching unsuspecting co-workers carrying out treatments on broomstick-and-pillow patients.

We got him back on his birthday one year. Six of us went to his house to kidnap his pride and joy: a pink plastic pig in his garden. He was soooo proud of her.

There we were, secretly trying to gain access to his back yard, when someone yelled, "Who's there?"

Darn it, caught in the act.

But luck was on our side as it was only his son, who became a willing accomplice.

Off we went, pink pig in the trunk. Ransom notes with pictures were sent on a weekly basis. Piggy was fried in a barbeque and photographed wearing a fuchsia negligee with black trim, a rose laying beside her on the bed, or tied helplessly to railway tracks as the train bore down. Pork hocks, fresh from the butcher, were sent to cause a ripple of fear in daddy's heart. We

spent many hours laughing over the escapades of this pig.

Finally the ransom request, for homemade pie and coffee, was agreed upon. A safe return of Miss Piggy was guaranteed.

When I take time for this kind of fun and laughter I feel refreshed and ready for the world.

One little trick I like to use to keep my smile going is 'toys.' I'm not too old to play! I have access to a supply of provocative playthings, thanks to a unit clerk who knew the importance of giggling. When banged, hit, or smashed, they emit noises that create a laughter inside that bubbles out across my face.

I recently discovered another funny creature on the counter in the Emergency Department: a 'jabberwoky' doll. It has a long, skinny neck, just right to clench a fist around. When shaken, it makes this garbled noise and I crack

up laughing. I borrowed it during a gruelling shift to lighten up the mood around the building. My crazy laughter spread like spilt urine on a freshly waxed floor.

> Laughter is a form of internal jogging. It moves your internal organs around. It enhances respiration. It is an igniter of great expectations.
>
> Norman Cousins

Mad: Anger Angst

Anger is an emotion that demands change and motion.

Unknown

Anger comes packaged in several layers: crabbiness, sarcasm, blowups and blowouts.

I need to be crabby sometimes, and it feels great. I snarl and snort and bang things around. In case people don't get it, I even tell them, "I'm bitchy today. Stay out of my way."

Crabs come in all shapes and sizes: big ones, little ones, chronically crabby and only occasionally crabby. Some crabs spend their whole career perfecting the role.

I finally 'got it' — my job is to control how I react to these toe biters, not try to fix them. As I had done for my own crabbiness, I acknowledged theirs.

"Oh, I see you're having a crabby day. I had mine last week; you must have missed it. It was one of my finer ones."

As I allow myself to be human, I do the same for those around me. I also notice that they have a hard time staying crabby alongside someone as goofy as me.

I do not remember being taught what to do with my anger. I was told never to show it, to learn to control it and don't even go there!

Anger stays stuck in me and eventually I explode. WOW! Take cover, run for your lives, because EXPLODE, I do.

And when the dust settles, I feel awful, yet no further ahead than when I was enraged. Well, maybe a bit of release occurs, but others around me are not happy about my outbursts.

Why does anger scare people?

I read where anger is one letter away from danger. I totally agree with this statement, yet I know that being angry is a human feeling. And I am going to and need to feel it.

I've been learning to let my anger out in healthier ways.

I allow myself to feel it for a specific length of time, then let it go.

I pound pillows for five or ten minutes, I play loud music in my car, and scream along with it, and — my all-time favorite — I smash old plates or glasses. I get a particular thrill out of this last one!

My mosaic masterpieces end up at the bottom of the basement stair. The act of cleaning and vacuuming adds to my release. Actually, by the time I descend the stairs, I am laughing at myself.

My anger with co-workers was one of the hardest problems I have dealt with. I allowed bickering about who works harder and who's not doing their fair share to take up far too much of my time. I found myself snorting around and banging cupboards, muttering under my breath and giving abrupt answers to questions. My physical cues screamed, "Boy, are you in trouble!"

I thought they were stupid and inconsiderate for not knowing what I needed. The fact that they were struggling in their own corner of hell eluded me.

Lacking the ability to communicate my needs and expectations created this atmosphere. I spent time working on changing the way I interact with fellow workers, telling them what I needed or wanted from them. Now I have more fun, and fewer conflicts at work.

Anger is a wind which blows out the lamp of the mind.

Robert Ingersoll

The blowups and blowouts are events that make the most hardened nurses cringe. I have observed these dramas throughout my career, and along with them, the variety of ways nurses respond.

What I have not seen, however, is an end to

this behavior! Someone is screaming in my face, unwanted, frightening, and uncomfortable — what do I do?

During a shift from hell, I had the dubious pleasure of working with a doctor who had been known for sporadic outbursts and berating of staff.

I was trying to handle six simultaneous verbal orders from this physician. I prioritized the orders in my head — or so I thought.

Soon I was being screamed at. "Why are you not doing this faster? Why did you pick that to do first? Where's your help?"

I looked across the patient and snapped at this annoying doctor, "If you wish me to do things in a different order, ask me. I ranked your orders how I thought was appropriate, and I only have two hands! So unless you wish to be the other pair of hands, I suggest you leave!"

To this day I have not had any similar encounters with this doctor. Was it hard to do? No.

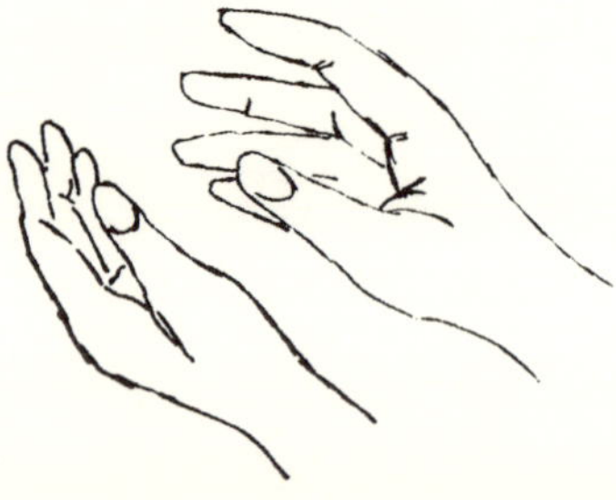

not when he was interfering with my patient's care. The protective part of me rose up in my throat and it became very easy to stand up for myself — and for my patient.

When I witness two people going at it, my stomach lurches up. I hate conflict. I know we are supposed to remove people from public view, yet I watch as everyone stands around with their eyes bulging, chins on the floor, wishing it would open up and swallow them. Some quickly escape the vicinity. Someone inevitably steps in, which often only escalates the dispute.

When finished with the explosion, these very same people carry on as if nothing happened. But now the person they have decimated is left to attempt to conduct business as usual. How do I stop this?

Some days I feel like an NHL goalie deflecting people's anger. It demands strong survival techniques.

Having a plan is crucial for me. I need

a list to cook by, so it figures that I need a list for everything else.

Over the last 25 years I have attended a couple of conflict management workshops, but the majority of my instruction has come from the good old-fashioned school of hard knocks.

I have mastered other skills, but this one will need lots of practice.

Having a plan allows me to feel less frustrated and more in control of myself. Now, each episode makes me stronger.

A.P.A.R.T.

Let us not look back in anger or forward in fear, but around in awareness.

James Thurber

A.P.A.R.T. — as in keeping apart from chaos — is a model I use to deal with my feelings and reactions. This acronym helps me remain focused on my patients.

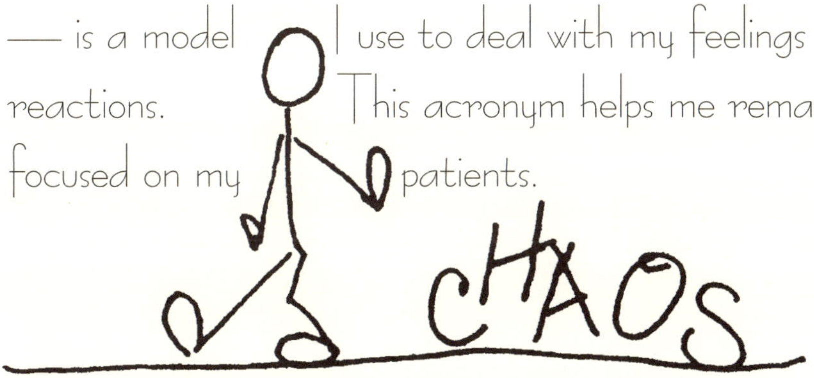

A.P.A.R.T. stands for Awareness, Plan, Action, Response, Trust. It allows me to choose to act, not react.

Acknowledging my feelings and being aware of their source is the first step. When I keep the patient at the center of my vocabulary and

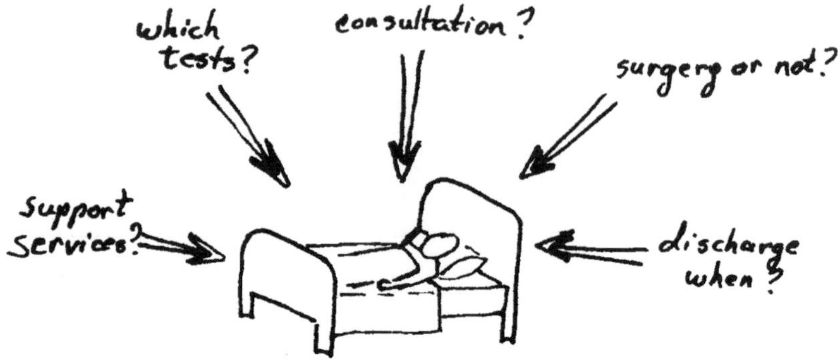

decisions, it helps me to develop a plan.

From this I choose a more appropriate action by keeping my emotions separate. Fresh responses to my actions lead me to trust my problem solving abilities.

One evening I entered the labor room and was greeted by a senior staff member who was visibly angry. She had spent her entire shift coaching and bonding with her patient only to have the doctor tell her he would coach the patient through her delivery.

"I am so mad I could spit nails," the nurse said. "I wish he would stop doing that."

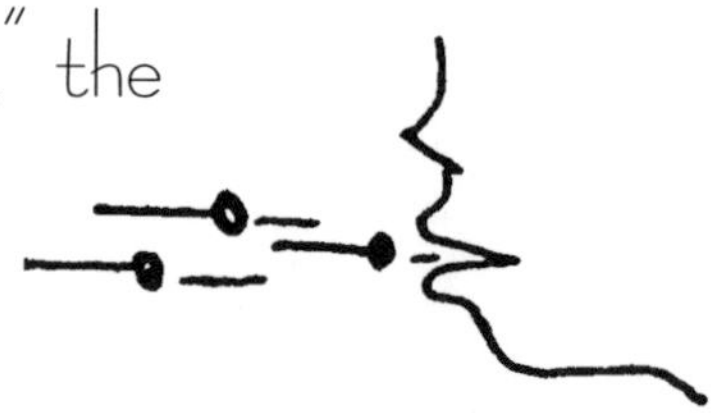

"What is really making you angry?" I asked, thinking it was because of the way the doctor had spoken to her.

The response was revealing. "I felt I abandoned my patient at the very time she needed me most," she said.

"We know that expecting the doctor to change is not going to happen," I said. "So who or what else can we change?"

We discussed preparing this physician's patients by informing them of his wishes to be their coach during delivery. We also knew we would need to reassure the patients that their nurse would stay with them for support.

A week later this same nurse excitedly told me that she had tried the new plan and that it had worked well. There was also a noticeable lessening of tension between her and the doctor. Interestingly, she asked me why she couldn't see that herself.

"You were too angry," I answered. "I was able to see it because my emotions were not involved." I had helped her step apart from the chaos, leaving her with a renewed sense of self-trust.

There are days when I really worry about

our profession. Everyone is working hard and is emotionally stressed.

I once sat down to have coffee with group of staff on an unusually quiet shift. After a bit of small talk, one the nurses turned to me and unloaded. On and on it went, about how badly he was being treated and how this co-worker was just jealous.

When the barrage stopped, I simply said, "Why do you care?"

He gave me a shocked look and his partner almost swallowed her teeth. I repeated my question and added, "Someone as smart as you should not care about how someone else sees you. It has been my experience that most of the time other people are too preoccupied with what you're thinking of them to be pursing any interest in your life. Even if they were, why would you care?"

I prefer to be in control of my emotions and reactions. This control creates a power. How I use my power — or if I chose to give it away

— is always under my control. This strategy takes practice, and I often falter.

I called one of the doctors to find out his plans for a patient waiting for surgery. What I received was a rant about his busy schedule and the inappropriate demands of this patient's family. When he was taking a breath, I calmly stated, "So you are not taking Mr. _ _ _ to the operating room today? Or perhaps for the next week?"

He snapped back, "YES, that's correct!"

"Fine thank you very much."

I ended the call, informed the charge nurse (the one hanging on every word of my side of the conversation) of the exchange, and she in turn talked to the family.

The family was furious, as we knew they would be. They had been sitting around for three days, waiting each day for the call to surgery, riding a roller coaster of emotions. Now we had ended that ride. A conversation with their family doctor who consulted another surgeon and their saga was over.

My point is that in the past I would have been angry at the doctor's tirade, taken it personally and entered into a verbal battle with no easy win. Now I am practicing a different approach that wins for my patients.

The staff kept saying, "Oh, what's Doctor so-and-so going to say? He's going to be so angry."

It is not my responsibility if that surgeon is upset about the patient being treated by a new doctor. He made his intentions known and must deal with the consequences.

Freedom is created by your ability to choose how you will act.

Anonymous

Complimentary Gratitude

A gift — be it a present, a kind word or a job done with care and love — explains itself, and if receivin' it embarrasses you, it's because your 'thanks box' is warped.

Alice Childress

I don't recall being taught what to say when someone said "thank you" to me. What I picked up from my observations of the replies of others was, "Oh, it was nothing," or "No thanks are necessary," or "You don't need to thank me, it's my job," or "No problem, anytime."

These eventually became my own acceptable responses. They were humble and polite.

But I never learned to simply say, "You're welcome."

My shushing, belittling and turning aside gratitude stopped me from accepting and receiving the true gift of a 'thank you'.

This was not just biting the hand that feeds me, this was also pushing it away!

I see now how disrespectful this was to the person thanking me and also to myself. My words carry so much meaning, yet they had made me feel degraded, devalued and insignificant. I was doing this to myself in the subconscious belief that this was what was acceptable and expected of me.

Learning to say "You're welcome" was a struggle. I stumbled and fumbled with it, and, at times, still do.

My first attempt, in a quavery, weak voice, was "You're welcome, but it was nothing." I thought this was better, yet it was really no different than before.

With practice I can now simply say, "You're welcome."

Being the chatty Kathy that I am, this is very hard. It is like saying "no" and nothing else. I constantly want to fill what I feel is a void of silence (there's my Rescuer mode shining through). Keeping my mouth shut after speaking is my test of fortitude and courage.

I now feel a great deal healthier emotionally and mentally. I am now hearing the words "thank you" and feeling truly appreciated by them.

Smiling, I reply with a gracious, "You're welcome."

These exchanges being simple, meaningful and honest.

Words and Other Meanings

... if we desire to communicate, that we must be careful about the words we use, for they may be using us! We can and must control our words... for the words we use will, in a very real sense, determine our beliefs systems and our actions. Use them rather than be used and narrowed by them!

Leo Buscaglia

Accurate and effective communication is a large part of my current position as hospital supervisor.

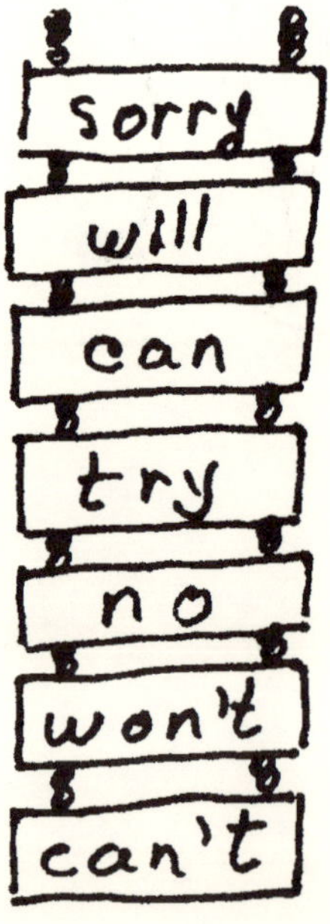

But proper word usage and clear communicating skills were not extensively taught in nursing school. These certainly would have helped me avoid word transmission pitfalls throughout my career. Through seminars, reading, and trial and error, I am learning!

Vanquishing 'I'm Sorrys'

You must do the thing you think you can not do.

Eleanor Roosevelt

The use of "I'm sorry" is flagrant, both in myself and by those around me. Once, when I prefixed my phone conversation with it, a doctor replied, "Then don't bother me," and hung up.

A friend who has worked overseas told me that constant apologizing is a Canadian trait. According to some nationalities she worked with, Canadians are sorry to be alive.

I started watching and realized how unconsciously I and others use those two little words.

Do you know how many times I say it in a hour?

"I'm sorry," is a virus in my vocabulary!

I seemed sorry for everything: when people waited, when someone bumped into me, when I needed to perform a procedure on a patient, and on and on.

Saying "I'm sorry, I need to give you this enema, or start this intravenous, or put down this nasogastric tube," is saying "I'm sorry, I have a job to do," or "I'm sorry I'm a nurse."

Does an electrician apologize when he shuts the power off to your house for an hour or two while he replaces some wiring?

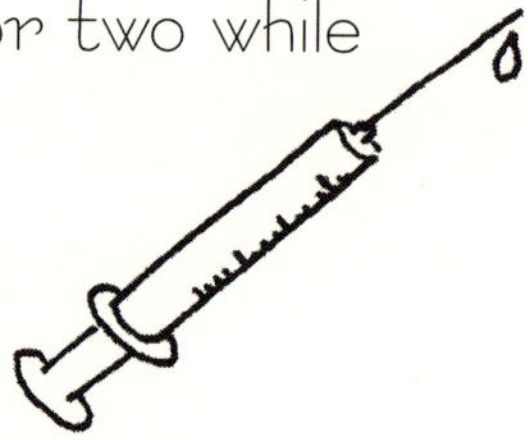

Does a dentist apologize for giving you freezing before doing a filling?

Then why do we as nurses continually apologize for our work?

I recently overheard a staff member use "I'm sorry" as her opening line in a phone conversation with a doctor. I asked her why she had said "I'm sorry." She was surprised and replied that she thought it indicated politeness.

It does no such thing! In fact it indicates selfishness as it brings the focus of the conversation to the nurse instead of the patient.

A doctor, overhearing this dialogue, jokingly observed that nurses are passive-aggressive. They ask for things passively and when they don't get them, they become aggressive.

These push/pull emotional encounters can be long and tiring. Too much time and energy are expended dealing with what could have been a two-minute problem. Often, in the end, the needs of the patient are not met.

Not apologizing in these types of conversations takes me out of the picture and puts the primary focus back on the patient. As I am more direct in my requests, patients' needs are met.

I realized my other "I'm sorrys" had become bland from misuse and overuse. I now practice not saying "I'm sorry" unless I am truly sorrowful. "I'm sorry, your father passed away," or "Your child died," or "You will not see from that eye again."

My sorrows are kept for genuinely sorrowful situations and my self-respect remains intact. As I expend less time and energy on the unnecessary "I'm sorrys," I have more for myself. I also have more of both for my patients.

Push Me — Pull Me

Language is our way of communicating what we want and who we are.

Dr Laura Schlessinger

Other words I have used, misused and bemoaned the results of are 'can/can't' and 'will/won't'.

Thinking before I speak so I am clear in what I want sounds so easy. Why isn't it?

I have the good fortune of having a teacher for a mother, one who loves the English language. When I asked, "Can you drive me downtown?" she would respond, "You do not mean 'can'. Can means 'am I able'. You should ask me if I 'will'."

So I should be an expert at this, right? Wrong!

"Can you get me the chart?"

"Can you answer the phone?" Using the wrong words creates a reaction from people. When used on me I feel unsettled and think they do not trust my abilities. For me it's mostly a careless unconscious habit, just like using "I'm sorry".

I am working to remove 'can' and 'can't' from my speech. When I truly do not have the ability to do something like, "I cannot make an elephant fly," or "I cannot build bunk beds," saying so will hold the strength of its meaning.

I am learning to say "I will" or "I won't" because there are very few things I can and can't do.

I think I can, I think I can, I think I can.

The Little Engine That Could

A 'Trying' Time

Character consists of what you do on the third and fourth tries.

Unknown

I think the word 'try' is a cop-out word. When I use it, it is not to say, "No, I will not," or "No, I cannot." It does not give a clear answer. Instead it causes confusion, especially in a workplace that runs on timed events.

"Barb, would you take the lady in bed 1-1 over for an x-ray?"

"I'll try and get to it."

Why couldn't she just say "Yes" or "No"? It would have been easier if she had given me a clear answer. Now I'm left waiting to see if she does it, doing it myself or finding someone else.

Now when I have a misunderstanding or obvious miscommunication, I think back to the words I used. Were they clear? Could they be taken a different way? It takes less time to do it right than to patch up the mistake.

Say "No", for the Health of It

I want to know if you can disappoint another to be true to yourself; if you can bear the accusation of betrayal and not betray your soul; if you can be faithless and therefore be trustworthy.

Oriah Mountain Dreamer

Working full time and juggling my role as nursing union president placed unbelievable demands on my time. I did not feel my life belonged to me. Learning to say "No" became a necessity.

The first real "No" was the hardest. I felt the guilt of letting someone down — I wanted to take the 'no' back. I knew I wouldn't, so why was I so mad? Why wouldn't they understand? Would they still trust me?

But I had honored my time and person.

I am also learning to say "No" without added

apologies, excuses or justifications. When I add these things I am rescuing the other person from their own feelings. A simple 'no' is enough and adding the rest weakens my 'no' and depletes me.

Just say "No" and let it go.

Caution: saying this tiny word causes others to stop and stare at you as if you've sprouted two heads. There are usually consequences for saying "no".

People balk: "What's wrong with you?" "What's going on?"

Have I said "yes" that often?

Their reaction is their responsibility, not mine. I need only worry about my shaky knees and sweaty palms.

Slowly, and with painful practice, it grew easier to say 'that' word.

Every 'no' is a 'yes' to myself, a 'yes' to my self-preservation and self-esteem. And those positive feelings trickle down to my family, friends and patients.

I must remind myself there are strategic 'no's' and insubordinate ones.

I flash common sense through my brain before I spew out my "no".

Have I died from saying "no"? Nope!

Did I disappoint people? I'm sure I did!

Am I healthy because of that word? You bet I am. Do I forget and say "yes" when I mean "no"? Sometimes, but not often anymore.

I say "no" when I want to say "no". I say "yes" when I want to say "yes". People may not like me but they respect me. I like myself more and respect myself more.

"No" is assertive, not aggressive. "No" is healthy. "No" needs no explanation.

Insubordinately Subordinate

Question with boldness even the existence of a God; because if there be one he must approve of the homage of reason more than that of blindfolded fear.

Thomas Jefferson

The dictionary is very succinct regarding the definition of insubordinate — it says 'disobedient'.

In our place of work I have looked at it this way. There are three groups of people I am accountable to: patients, my professional organization, and my employer. If my first accountability is to the patients and their safety, my professional code of ethics will not be placed in jeopardy.

Those who think it's your job to listen to their authority use the term 'insubordinate' when you stand up for your professional accountability. I had just such an incident as a fairly new nurse and a new employee in an intensive care unit.

In the wee night hours during a snowstorm, a newly admitted medical patient's heart stopped. I was the 'code' nurse for that shift and off I went pushing and pulling on the 'old red tool box' on wheels we used for a 'crash cart'. There was no doctor 'in house', so I was in charge of the 'code'. I confidently put to use my recently acquired knowledge from an Advanced Cardiac Life Support course. The night supervisor arrived as I was following the algorithms. She mumbled a couple of things and left the room. A few minutes later she returned, and told the orderly doing chest compressions to stop.

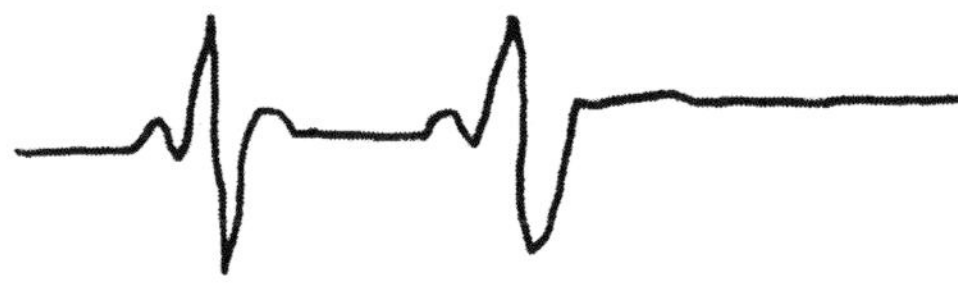

"Excuse me?" I asked.

"There's no point, the doctor can't make it in because of the storm," she stated.

I was very upset with her, as I did not believe she had received a doctor's order to stop the code.

The orderly looked like he was watching a tennis match. His eyes darted back and forth between the supervisor and myself. She was yelling as I went to phone the doctor. He confirmed that he could not make it out of his driveway and asked me if there were any signs of life from the patient. I told him that I had gone through the standard drug protocol with this patient and still no signs of life. He gave me a phone order to end the 'code'.

My night was just beginning as I had challenged my supervisor's authority and she was as mad as a wet hen. Following me back to the intensive care unit, she proceeded to yell more. Finally I'd had enough and demanded she leave me alone. Her commotion was also disturbing the patients.

Can you guess what happened next? Yes! I received a phone call around 0830 hours just as I started to nod off in my warm bed. I was standing in my director's office early that afternoon answering a charge of insubordination. I refused to agree and argued that blindly following her orders would have caused me to breach policy and place my licence on the line. Common sense ruled and I came away facing no disciplinary action and no further problems from that supervisor.

The words 'disobedient' and 'doctors' often rang together in my head. I no longer allow the ringing to go on. I know doctors are not my masters. They work with me! The belief about their right to order staff around still exists in today's settings. I have seen it paralyze nurses, preventing them from standing up for themselves and — ultimately — their patients.

I was one of these nurses. I allowed it. I owe no one my obedience. I am now unwilling to consider the worry of getting in trouble for questioning a course of treatment for a patient. I confront doctors and managers.

I am practicing the art of nursing, not insubordination.

Shining It Forward

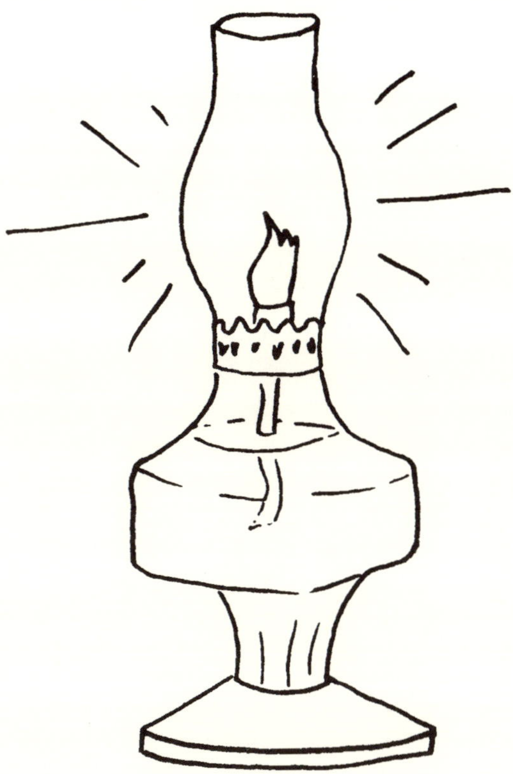

The Nurses' Bill Of 'Wills'

1. We will respect ourselves through thoughts, words and actions, treating others with identical respect.
2. We will express our true feelings and opinions.
3. We will say "No", without feeling the need for justification or guilt.
4. We will ask for what we need.
5. We will make mistakes. We are hopelessly human, after all.
6. We will be ourselves, different than others may want us to be.
7. We will be paid fairly for our work.
8. We will continue to learn.
9. We will work in a safe and caring environment.
10. We will practice professional ethics, with the patient as our prime focus.

11. We will be an equal member of the health-care team.

12.

13.

We leave these blanks for your 'willing' contributions.

Strength does not come from physical capacity. It comes from an indomitable will.

Mahatma Gandhi

Advisory

A ship in port is safe but that is not what ships are built for.
Unknown

There are perils on the high seas, and this overhaul journey causes adverse reactions in others as well as myself.

Hyperventilation may occur; keep a little brown

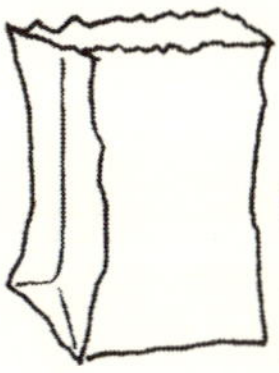

bag ready — also handy for seasickness. Grip-soled shoes may help maintain your balance during stormy waters. (Ah ha!) That's where the term 'get a grip' comes from.

My yellow rain hat and slicker are with me at all times, along with life preservers and goggles. Kleenex tissues are a must for this passage, and fluffy soft towels serve a dual purpose.

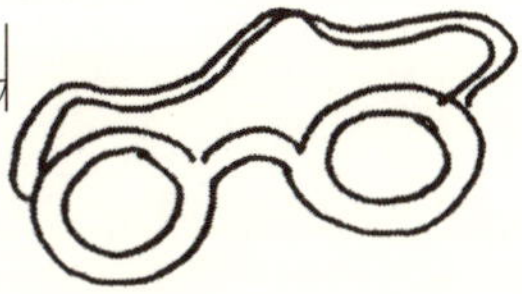

Some folks keep trying to pull me back to shore, often throwing lifelines I no longer want. They act

angry and strange, all the while accusing me of a sundry of things. To them, I must seem crackers as I break away from old patterns and habits. I have lost friends but gained new ones. Mostly I have made people think.

At times, I want to turn back, anxious to stand on old, familiar ground but knowing that old land was not the healthiest for me. When the going gets rough, I falter, staying in my cabin and not venturing out on deck. Old habits get tossed overboard as I adjust new ones to fit. Not surprisingly, those old ones often are swept, wave-like, back into my life and I begin again to hoist my sails.

And what a ride I am having! I am learning to traverse the seas with humanness and at my own speed.

A licence to practice nursing is your ticket to ride.

Welcome aboard.

Bon voyage.

Whatever you think you can do or believe you can do, begin it. Action has magic, grace and power in it.

Goethe

Finessing the Future

So many of our dreams at first seem impossible then they seem improbable, and then when we summon up the will they soon become inevitable.

Christopher Reeve

In all the places I have worked I wanted one common thing: to know I was valued as an individual and as part of the team, for my intelligence and abilities.

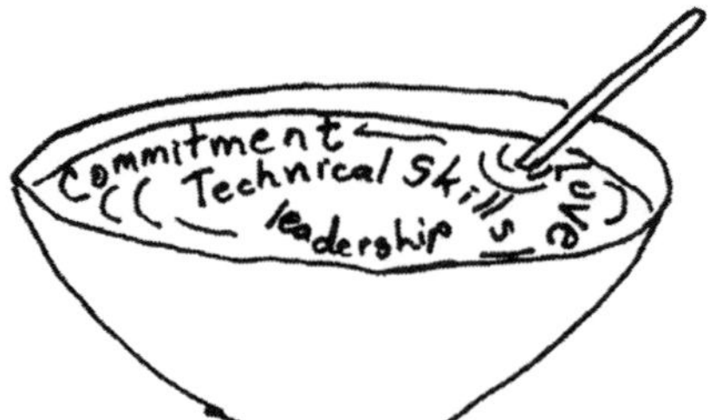

The question I have for myself is, what do I want and need in order to continue to nurse? What do I dream?

I want to pass on my love and commitment to nursing, and the importance of a mix of technical skills coupled with leadership skills.

My colleagues have told me it is difficult to mentor others, and not all wish to take on this challenging role. If only they could see themselves as I see them: strong, caring, intelligent and more than able to serve as a role model for new staff.

I sense a need to encourage the present staff. Nurses must look for inventive ways to build bonds while creating a healthier workplace.

Nursing basics are taught at school. Developing finesse happens on the job. A nurse is only as strong as his or her knowledge of their environment, their colleagues, their contact and resource personnel. This strength is what makes senior nurses so valuable on their own units. They provide a wealth of knowledge not easily assessable to the less-experienced staff.

Early in my role of supervisor I received a page on my beeper from a medical unit. The time was 2315 hours — shift change. Oh, oh! I said to myself. Sure enough, there was a no-show for the night shift. One of the new graduates had encountered trouble figuring out the schedule.

Each group of new hires add gray hairs to my locks. Tracking this particular nurse down was like watching a detective movie. She had recently married, and the staff had no new phone number or address for her. No one knew her parents, or if she was even from the city or lived in a nearby rural area. A senior nurse saved us from drowning in our own pool of despair as her hairdresser turned out to be a close relative of this young gal. Now it was 2330, and being desperate, I took the plunge and dialed the number. We had solved the mystery.

I envision a system where each new hire is paired with a senior staffer, acting as a big brother or big sister. They are responsible to help them navigate through the invisible but emotion-laden expectations of the job. An environment of trust and respect is created when the new staff can learn to avoid the hidden potholes.

Sitting on a break with other staff recently I listened to them talk about their work. One of the undergrads stated she'd had no idea how physically demanding nursing was. They spoke of their first year of nursing and how scary it had been.

I told them that in my last year of nursing training I had also worked as an undergrad. On the unit I had become close to the staff and they were pushing me to apply for a position after graduation. The manager on this unit was very stern and old fashioned: No gum, pressed uniforms, clean shoes.

There was the stickler. My shoes were scuffed and worn out, three years of nursing training evident in their condition.

Having little in the way of money as my scholarship fund had dwindled away, I had no intention of buying new shoes until graduation. Unbeknown to me, a group of the staff got together and bought me a new pair of shoes. The manager was returning from holidays and they wanted me to make a good first impression upon her, in the hope that she would hire me.

This kind of care and concern from people who I worked with gave me such strength and confidence. I felt I could conquer the world.

Mentors

by Linda Bridge

One little word
Unable to replace
No other comparable
What once commonplace
We take for granted
The effort it took
To bring us along
Knowing only the book
My life has been blessed
Mentors great ones too few
They do not happen everyday
It's fortunate I got YOU

After finishing my story I went on to talk about the 'big sister' program we had in my school. I told them how being a big sister was not only helpful to the little, but to the big sister as well. They were excited and asked if they could start something like that. Would they need permission from their manager?

I was thrilled and I told them they did not need permission to treat each other well.

I have noticed that there is an unspoken way to work on each unit. Who knows who invented it? Lord help those who do not find out what it is. If this code of conduct had been spelled out, my life would have been oh so much simpler. It was clearly something I just expected a 'good nurse' to know.

On my dream unit there would be an emotion station in each staff room, full of creative ways to release bottled-up emotions. I feel strongly that we need to take care of ourselves and each other.

Some simple solutions that do not need a lot of space would help: A locked box with a pad of paper where staff can write down anything they want to — anger, grief, wishes, dreams, frustrations, it doesn't matter. No one will read them. Just throw away or burn the box when it's full.

Ok, ok, quit laughing. It's not everyone, but for those who are smirking I have a blow-up punching bag. A few humor books like The Blue Day Book: A Lesson in Cheering Yourself Up © 2000 Bradley Trevor Grieve. How about a set of Magnetic Poetry: words for creative and fun thoughts on your refrigerator? With some creative thinking there can be an amazing number of ideas generated. The point is to go for it!

Do you need permission from a manager? Why would they say "no" to a healthier staff?

If you find your punching bag deflated or stuck in a corner, bring it out and blow it back up. Eventually it will be left alone.

When a critical or upsetting situation happens on your unit, allow those involved a small break away to collect themselves. We are not machines, even if we act like we are.

I need just to be quiet for five or ten minutes after a 'code'. Not having to smile or be polite for those few minutes recharges my energy.

Memories wash over me. Vivid colors of a blue baby blanket wrapped up around a blue, cold child who died of SIDS. The mother with blank, dark eyes not seeing anything, just holding this bundle. I walked out from behind the curtains to an angry man yelling in my face about the pain in his ear, "Where the hell is the doctor?" I did not respond, but just walked on by.

Running from crisis to crisis does not allow for 'time out' to acknowledge and deal with our feelings. Missing this brief opportunity to purge them only creates a greater need later on.

Savor the 'I'

Savor: giving oneself to the enjoyment of; power to excite or interest.

Webster's Dictionary

I allowed myself to be socially programmed to believe my commitment was to others; my job was a self-sacrifice.

I created my own pedestal and appointed myself a savior — a rescuer of all.

My ears were plugged with righteous cotton and I could not hear the words, "Save your own butt."

Many years passed before I stumbled upon my tarnished old lamp, precariously dangling from my pedestal. I was humbled at the sight of it.

But I was truly excited to find my lamp and realized I had a vested interest in polishing it. The 'hows' of installing a new wick were daunting, but based on simple strategies .I held my nose and jumped from my pedestal.

I separated 'I' out of savior, and began to savor the 'I'.

Often others in our lives are relieved when we stop giving ourselves away.

Being a *hopelessly human* nurse is not self-centered or heartless. Being a *hopelessly human* nurse is being aware of my true value as a person, and becoming a happier, healthier, more loving and caring ME.

Welcome

by Kathy Knowles

You are a hero, your courage limitless. I welcome you to trust in your bravery and create your happiness.

You have a bounty of credentials. I welcome you to peel back your layers, allowing the world to admire and appreciate your humanness.

What are your dreams? And will you risk others' wrath to live your wildest ones?

Infinite pleasure from nature's simple rewards awaits. I welcome you to let it touch you, in the millisecond your eyes blink when you drive to work.

You are the perfect shape, the perfect size, and the perfect color. I welcome you to stand in front of the mirror and see what I and others see: your tremendous beauty, worth and greatness.

Why are you trying to keep up with the Joneses?

Will you accept yourself and all of the world?

I welcome you to end the selfish "I'm sorrys." Believe in your personal goodness and pamper it silly!

Will you laugh with me, cry with me, live with me, die with me? Or will you shut me down and turn me off from feeling my true feelings. . . chastising me for being alive?

I want to know what you know. Do you know what I know? Together, let's encourage growth and learning, moving forward in our knowledge of life.

You need not accept or approve of me but I welcome you to approve of yourself.

And will you overhaul your lamp to become a *hopelessly human* nurse?

P.I.F.*

*Permissions, Interests and Forever Gratefuls

Permissions

Linda and Kathy thank the following publishers and authors who gave permission to reprint writings from their selected works:

A Return To Love, Marianne Williamson, 1992, reprinted by permission of HarperCollins Publishers Inc. Portions reprinted from *A Course In Miracles,* 1975, by Foundation for Inner Peace, Inc. All chapter openings from A Course In Miracles.

Medical-Surgical Nursing: A Psychophysiologic Approach, Luckman, Joan and Sorensen, Karen, pg. 15, 1974, reprinted by permission of Elsevier.

Autobiography In Five Short Chapters, pp. 44-45, from *There's A Hole In My Sidewalk,*

Nelson, Portia, 1993, reprinted by permission of Beyond Words Publishing Inc.

Women Who Run With The Wolves, Pinkola Estes, Clarissa, 1992, published by Ballantine Books, a subsidiary of Random House, Inc.

Loving Each Other, Buscaglia, Leo, pp. 118, 1984, reprinted by permission of SLACK Inc.

The Invitation, Mountain Dreamer, Oriah, 1999, reprinted by permission of HarperCollins Publishers Inc.

Express permission was received from Stephen Karpman PhD, for the use of his 'drama triangle' concept. The Persecutor, Rescuer and Victim are roles which are part of people's daily social games. Karpman pointed out to the authors that the triangle can also be used for the inner drama within ourselves; i.e., a person feels bad (V), Rescues themselves by overeating, then Persecutes themselves for doing it, then feels bad (V), and starts the cycle all over again.

We acquired the concepts, which are used in the chapter, 'The Healthier Triangle' (also known as the 'winner's triangle'), from Betty Kendall RN, BScN, a therapist who uses Transactional Analysis (TA). The concept of the four 'true' feelings (mad, sad, glad and fear) was taught by TA therapist, Maisie Jacobson during the course, 'Who am I'. Terminology and concepts used or adapted with their respective permissions.

'Welcome' pp. 152-153 was inspired by the prose poem 'The Invitation' by Oriah Mountain Dreamer from her book of the same name.

Attempts were made to trace the original source of quotes and concepts used within this book. If errors or omissions are found by copyright holders, please contact the publisher.

INTERESTS

We share with you the following books that over the past few years helped us to get to where we are today.

- Achterberg, Jeanne. *Woman Healer: a panoramic survey of the healing activities of women from prehistoric times to the present.* Boston: Shambhala Publications, 1990.
- Buresh, Bernice and Gordon, Suzanne. *From Silence to Voice: What Nurses Know and Must Communicate to the Public.* Ottawa: Canadian Nurses Association, 2000.
- Buscaglia, Leo. *Living, Loving & Learning.* New York: Ballantine Books, 1982.
- —. *Loving Each Other: The Challenge of Human Relationships.* New Jersey: SLACK Incorporated, 1984.
- Cameron, Julia. *The Artist's Way: A Spiritual Path to Higher Creativity.* New York: G. P. Putnam's Sons, 1992.

• Clemmer, Jim. *GROWING the distance: Timeless principles for personal, career, and family success.* Kitchener: TCG Press, 1999.

• Corcoran, Barbara and Littlefield, Bruce. *If you don't have big breasts, put ribbons on your pigtails: and other lessons I learned from my mom.* New York: Penguin Books Ltd., 2003.

• Donahue, M. Patricia. *Nursing: The Finest Art. An Illustrated History.* St. Louis: The C.V. Mosby Company, 1985.

• Dooley, Mike. *Notes from the Universe: new perspectives from an old friend.* Orlando: Totally Unique Thoughts, 2003.

• Faber, Adele and Mazlish, Elaine. *How to Talk So Kids Will Listen & Listen So Kids Will Talk.* New York: Rawson, Wade Publishers, Inc., 1980.

• G. & C. Merriam Co. *The Merriam-Webster Dictionary.* New York: Simon & Schuster, Inc., 1974.

• Grieve, Bradley Trevor. *The Blue Day Book: A Lesson in Cheering Yourself Up.* Kansas City: Andrews McMeel Publishing, 2000.

- —. *The Meaning of Life.* Kansas City: Andrews McMeel Publishing, 2002.
- —. *Tomorrow: Adventures in an Uncertain World.* Kansas City: Andrews McMeel Publishing, 2003.
- Hay, Louise L. *You Can Heal Your Life.* Carlsbad, Hay House, Inc., 1984, 1987.
- Joines, Vann and Stewart, Ian. *TA Today: A New Introduction to Transactional Analysis.* Nottingham and Chapel Hill: Lifespace Publishing, 1987.
- Jones, Laurie Beth. *The Path: Creating your Mission Statement for Work and Life.* New York: Hyperion, 1996.
- Kemper, Dave, Meyer, Verne and Sebranek, Patrick. *Writers Inc: A Guide to Writing, Thinking, & Learning.* Burlington: Write Source Educational Publishing House, 1992.
- Luckmann, Joan & Sorensen, Karen. *Medical - Surgical Nursing: A Psychophysiologic Approach.* Philadelphia: W. B. Saunders Company, 1974.

• Macrorie, Ken. *Telling Writing* (third edition). New Jersey: Hayden Book Company, Inc.,1980.

• Mason, John L. *Let Go of Whatever Makes You Stop.* Tulsa: Insight Publishing, 1994.

• Mountain Dreamer, Oriah. *The Invitation.* New York: Harper San Francisco, 1999.

• Nichols, V. *Webster's Thesaurus: Dictionary Format.* USA: Nickel Press, 1992.

• Pinkola Estes, Clarissa. *Women Who Run With the Wolves: Myths and Stories of the Wild Woman Archetype.* New York: Ballantine Books, 1992.

• SARK. *Succulent Wild Woman: Dancing with your Wonder-full Self.* New York: Simon and Schuster, 1997.

• Scott, Claire. *Dare to Dream: A Survival Guide for Self-Publishers.* Calgary: Butterfly Blessings, 2000.

Forever Grateful

Many minds and hands contributed to the production of this book and to all, thank you.

To Rosalie, a talented artist and good friend, love from the depth of our souls.

We thank those who when asked for advice or material, so graciously supplied it; Betty Kendall, Alison Martin, Bonnie Sturm, Maisie Jacobson, Sheila Bailey and Bryan Deleske.

We are grateful for the tremendous encouragement and support from family, friends and colleagues.

To John, Keith, Christian, Darcy, Carmen, Jill, Dave, Rob, and Paul: We are honored to work with you. Thank you for your unique talents, attributes and especially your patience.